"Summerfest" is mentioned a number of times in this book. For those of you who are unfamiliar, it is the world's largest music festival and is held on the shores of Lake Michigan in downtown Milwaukee for 11 days from late June to early July each summer.

*To protect audio tracks from plagiarism, complete audio tracks known as "Audio Audacities" will be released to everyone who purchased this book after the first 100,000 copies are sold. All audio tracks will be available at that time at bangheader.com. Go to the soundtrack link and enter the password crazyhilariousaudacities In the meantime, short soundbytes from some of these tracks are now available at bangheader.com in the soundbyte link. Enjoy!

About The Author

Jerry Bangheader has lived his life as a rebel, adventurer, risk taker, explorer, entrepreneur, criminal, volunteer, and a lover of people, partying, and music. He seeks fun, challenges, knowledge and new experiences and enjoys being a day tripper and a night owl. He has a wealth of unique, unusual, dramatic, funny, and interesting experiences which he will share with you as well as his original sayings known as Jerryisms and his take on life. Fasten your seat belt. You're in for a wild ride.

Why The Dude Times Two

I call myself, "The Dude Times Two" because I drink Blind Russians which are all booze except the ice unlike, "The Dude" who drinks White Russians which are not all booze. I first enjoyed drinking Blind Russians when I was in my early twenties. They have been my favorite drink ever since. This delicious yet potent concoction keeps me feeling just right when I'm out at night however they are not your mother's Mudslide. If you decide to try them do so with respect. They may go down like chocolate milk but they can kick like a mule and if you drink too many you could get blindsided.

Bangheader's Badass Blind Russian Recipe

Fill a rocks glass with medium size ice cubes. Add 40% of your favorite unflavored vodka, 30% of your favorite coffee liquor, and 30% of your favorite Irish cream liquor. Mix well. If you want it to be a little stronger add more vodka. If you want it to taste more like coffee add more coffee liquor. If you want it to taste more like Irish cream liquor add more of that. Experiment and find what trips your taste buds. As long as you use only the ingredients listed above it is a Bangheader approved Badass Blind Russian.

Contents

Quick Picture Guide

Some of the pictures in this book as well as some bonus pictures and select concert ticket stubs may all be viewed in color at bangheader.com Go to the pictures link and enter password bangheaderspics

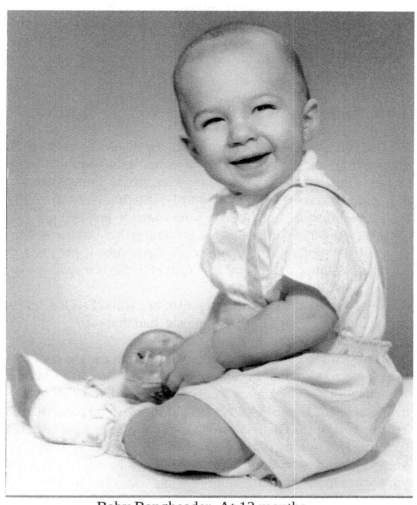

Baby Bangheader- At 13 months

Quick Audio Audacities Guide

This guide puts each audio track in context and the page of the book that it corresponds to. All of these messages were left on my voice mail. Some of the names and voices have been altered to protect the guilty.

Track Number   **Back Story**   **Page Number**

1-5 Larry Lashes Out- Unhappy with the results he was   105 getting from my dating service, these messages were all left in one evening. Yes, he did have a resemblance to Frankenstein.

6-7   Coreen Careens Out Of Control- After not paying   157 their rent, infesting my property with roaches, and being told when the the exterminator was coming, her boyfriend allegedly entered the apartment while the bombs were going off, had a asthma attach, and was rushed to the hospital. I never heard from her "lawyer."

8. Melanie Mouths Off- Tenants response when I called   179 her about a dog I didn't even know she had that was running loose in the common hallway.

9. Stinky Smell Hell- Tenant complains about the smell of marijuana coming into his apartment.   None

10. Diabolical Dick claims someone plastered notes all over his vehicle and describes what he was going to do about it. 183

11-13   Diabolical Dick- I caught him parking in a parking 196 spot that was not his When I called him on it he raised his voice and started mouthing off. That's when I said, "don't raise your voice to me chump." These are his responses to my statement. On message #11 he claims to be fifty two years old when he was actually forty eight. On message #13 he claims he is entitled to two parking spaces but his lease did not guarantee him any parking spaces.

To completely appreciate Diabolical Dick's messages read, The
Players In The Big Showdown, The Big Showdown, She's
Back, Wait There's More, and Dick's Last Stand before
listening to these messages. Dick did not move out or followed
through on any of the other threats he made in his messages.

11

Bangheader's Beliefs

1. My Religion And Philosophy In Life: Treat Your Fellow Human Being, All Other Living Things, And Your Mother Earth As Good Or Better Than You Would Like To Be Treated Yourself.

2. Life Is Full Of Choices. Ponder And Make Each One Wisely, Because Most Will Affect Your Happiness Either Negatively Or Positively.

3. Men- How To Have A Great Relationship: Treat Her Like Your Queen, Bring Home The Bacon, And Keep Your Dick In Your Pants. Ladies- How To Have A Great Relationship: Treat Him Like Your King, Bring Home The Bacon, And Save All Your Loving For Him.

4. If You Think Changing Partners Will Solve Your Relationship Problems, Remember You Will Just Be Exchanging A Set Of Problems You Are Familiar With For One That You Are Not, Because Nobody Is Perfect. This does not apply if you are in an abusive relationship.

5. Physical Fighting Is The Lowest Form Of Conflict Resolution.

6. If You're Doing One Thing That Is Illegal Don't Do Anything Else Illegal.

7. The Biggest Lie Of Mankind: We're All In This Together. The Capitalist Extrapolists Will Tell You Anything They

Think You Want To Hear So They Can Suck Every Last Dime Out Of You.

8. You Can't Please All Of The People All Of The Time But With A Little Effort You Can Please Most Of The People Most Of The Time.

9. In The Past, If Someone Was Looking Down And Didn't Go When The Lights Turned Green, You Could Be Pretty Sure That They Were Packing A Bowl. Now You Have To Try To Guess If They're Doing That, Texting, Or Playing A Video Game.

10. RE: Bangheader's Badass Blind Russian- Pour It And They Will Come.

Jerryisms- Jerry Bangheader's Original Sayings

1. I've Been Dunked In Your Skunk Till I Stunk.

2. My Main Chow Is Chow Mein.

3. How Much Do I Do? As Little As Possible, As Much As I Can.

4. It's Better To Invest A Dime Early Than A Dollar Late.

5. Too Much Of A Good Thing Can Make You Do Bad Things.

6. It's Not A Party Until Someone Gets Hurt Or Something Gets Broken.

7. Ozzy Rules All Others Must Pay Cash.

8. When You Run With The Best You Can Forget The Rest.

9. The Old Saying Went, " Spare The Rod And Spoil The Child." I Say, Spoil The Rod And Spare The Child.

10. Are You One Of A Kind Or Kind Of A One.

11. RE: Littering Glass- Break The Glass, You're An Ass.

12. Make Your Disability An Opportunity To Showcase Your Abilities.

13. I Prefer My Culture Live And I Get Most Of It In My Yogurt.

14. WTA- White Trash Antics

15. TBO- Taste Bud Orgasm

16. VCR- Verbal Communication Refuser. - A Friend Or Relative Who Does Not Return Calls.

17. Bagels And Donuts Or As I Like To Call Them Hole Foods.

18. Don't Do As I Do Or As I Say. If You Do, Do So Completely At Your Own Risk.

19. If You're Low Just Grab Your Mo Jo And Go Go Go.

20. My Rod And My Staff Shall Guide Me.

21. There May Be A Sucker Born Every Minute But There's A Fool Born Every Second.

22. It's Not A Question Of If There Will Be A Problem, But When.

23. You Thought You Were All That But You're Just A Bag Of Chips.

24. You Don't Have A Penis You Wouldn't Understand, or You Don't Have A Vajayjay You Wouldn't Understand.

25. If There's A Catch They're Probably Sketch or If Their Story's A Stretch They're Probably Sketch.

26. Give Credit Where Credit Is Due, Otherwise Cash Only.

27. You Are Morally Corrupt And Emotionally Bankrupt.

28. Wisdom Should Come With Age, Unfortunately Not All Who Get Old Become Wise.

29. It's Not Bragging If You Really Did It.

On Going To Bed Early and Staying Up Late

30. The Early Bird May Get The Worm But The Night Owl Gets To Scream and Howl.

31. If You're Up Late At Night You're Doing It Right.

32. Closed The Bar Without A Scar.

33. Early To Bed And Early To Rise Leaves A Person Sleepy And Tired Needing Stimulants To Survive.

Jerry Bangheader's Original Bumper Sticker Sayings.

1. I'll Get Off Your Ass Just Let Me Pass

2. If You Own The Road May I Borrow The Passing Lane For 10 Seconds

3. Down By The Floor On The Right- That's The Gas Pedal- STEP ON IT!

4. Move Over Exit Or Desist

5. Whoever Taught You How To Drive Should Give You Your Money Back

6. Did Someone Die Or Do You Always Drive Like You're In A Funeral Procession

7. Baby Board Me

Here Comes Trouble

On a cold November morning, my mother delivered me kicking and screaming into this world. Unlike my sisters, who came along a few years later, I was very vocal about my needs. It is told that I screamed frequently and furiously until those needs were met.

When I was two and a half, my mother needed to run down to the basement to do some laundry. She told me to wait for her in the living room. When she came back, I was gone... to be found a half block away following the garbage truck down the street wearing nothing but my underpants.

At four, my mom found me almost a block away, dressed in my winter clothing with my lunch bag in my hand. She asked, "Jerry, where are you going?" I seriously answered, "To the office."

At five, during a big thunderstorm, I bolted from a large meeting tent at the campground where our religion held their summer statewide meetings. I went to the building where my sisters' meeting was, collected them, and escorted them back to our cabin.

In a park I saw a sign that said, "No Dogs Allowed" and started laughing uncontrollably. My mom asked, "Jerry, what is so funny?" I replied, "Mother, everybody knows dogs can't read."

My kindergarten teacher told my mother that I wasn't going to amount to much and would probably end up in prison because I had my own ideas about everything. On Valentines Day she instructed the class to draw a heart. I drew my version of an eagle!

 At eight, my behavior or ability to learn my piano lessons as well as expected was not good enough for my teacher. I was ordered to hold my hand out so she could punish me with the ruler. Yes, I really did experience "Glory, Glory, Hallelujah! Teacher Hit Me With The Ruler!"

At our church grade school, we were required to finish all of our food before we could go out for recess. I was the culprit who snuck his government-issued, nasty cheddar cheese out of the cafeteria and ditched it on the stairs on my way out. The teacher said we wouldn't get to go out for recess again until the person who left it confessed. I kept my mouth shut and when recess time came she relented.

One day at home a baby sitter was watching me. I was wondering what would happen if I spit on the large light bulb in a floor lamp in the living room. The sitter stepped outside for a minute and I did it. It blew up! I was so afraid of what she would do that I locked her out of the house for hours.

At 10, I had my first girlfriend in fourth grade. She wrote me a note that said "The boys are trying to get me but I like you, not them," and enclosed a lock of her horse's hair! That summer her family moved away and we lost contact. Then La Donna moved in next door. We became fast flirts and she taught me how to make out. She was good at it, too. Her mom was divorced and I think La Donna learned by covertly watching her mom when she had a date over.

Around the age of 11, I started stealing from my mom and the store. She would send me down the block to the grocery store a couple of times a week. I would steal candy from the Brach's display or buy myself a couple of donuts, eating them on the way home and throwing away the receipt. I even graduated to stealing small cans of Hershey's chocolate syrup, hiding them in my bedroom and drinking it straight up. They don't make small cans like that anymore. They cost just ten cents.

That same year my friend and I threw a couple of erasers at each other in 5th grade geometry class. Our teacher, Mr. Cummings, saw us and we were called up in front of the class. He grabbed us both by our hair and banged our heads on the blackboard while yelling," You're gonna learn this now." My dad was so angry after hearing about it that it took all the reasoning mom could muster to keep him from going down and getting a piece of Mr. Cummings. In today's world, I am sure I would have been diagnosed with ADD.

Dad did like to drink. It wasn't a regular thing but about once a month he would go out on a bender, crashing the car, getting into a fight, or falling down breaking his nose and/or glasses. He only had one leg, so when he came home drunk and belligerent and fell on the floor, mom would take his crutches away so he couldn't chase her around.

I do have some pretty good memories of him when he was sober. He used to take me to the coffee shop where I would get a glass of soda and a donut or toast. It was a big deal to stare through the glass of the donut display in the counter and decide whether to get the Long John, cruller, or chocolate donut. Then there was the toast. Trying all the different jelly flavors was pretty exciting for me since we didn't use jelly at home. If his friend Ernie Brown took us in his T-Bird, I knew I could order anything I wanted and Ernie would pick up the tab. In those joyous moments, I usually ordered a strawberry malt and a chicken dinner. As a family, we rarely ate out and when we did it was at a pizza parlor, so those were very special occasions. We lived in an upper flat on 28th and Kilbourn, just a few blocks from the apartment where Jeffrey Dahmer committed his atrocities a number of years later. One of my friends even came face to face with Dahmer while Dahmer was with one of the people he killed.

When the civil rights riots, or race riots as we called them hit Milwaukee in July of 1967, my friend and I watched tanks roll down 27th St. and saw The National Guard snipers on top of the tower on the roof of The Telephone Company from our attic window. The whole city was under a 24 hour curfew and the police vehicles had tape on all of their windows so their glass would not fly if someone threw a brick. When the stores did open, there would be just 1-2 hours to get there and buy the food we needed.

About this time, my testosterone must have started kicking in. My antics included telling my mom that I would be sitting with my friend in the balcony at church. We would then skip out and go set off crude smoke bombs we had made, or go to Big Boy's, or the cafeteria at St. Mary's Hospital and spend our offering money on breakfast. I am not sure if it was because we looked so young or were dressed so well but we always got a big discount at the latter. A couple of times we played " the dine and dash card" by running out of Big Boy's without paying. After that, we would sneak up to the balcony and read the underground newspapers we picked up while out and about. I guess I took after my grandpa. It is told that he would tell people, "I'll see you in church if you're sitting by the window!"

<u>Never A Dull Moment In My Neighborhood</u>
Our neighborhood had an interesting mix of characters including the family next door. The father would frequently fall asleep with a burning cigarette, starting his mattress on fire and the fire department would come.

Down the street, crazy Sheboygan Betty had many, many cats. She and Old Man John, who was a Russian immigrant, lived together. She would sit on her porch getting drunk and yell at anyone nearby, frequently propositioning men walking past. We used to taunt Old Man John by throwing stones at him over his backyard fence. He would spray us with his hose and, eventually, he connected a steel pipe to the end so he could spray harder and further. One time Betty was mad at John and got some guys from down the street to come and beat him. They had him down on the ground in front of his house and were kicking him until the cops came. A few friends and I would get our kicks at night by knocking over garbage cans in the neighborhood and running off.

<u>As A Teen I Was Not A Good Dream</u>
At 12, I was baptized and joined our church mostly to go along with what the rest of my classmates in the 5th grade were doing. At 13, I asked to have my name removed from the church roster and formed a group we called "The Troublesome Trio" with two church friends. At summer camp, we pulled the breakers and shut off the power to part of the camp, shoved

rolls of toilet paper down the toilets to clog them, and threw rocks at nearby Amtrak trains. One of us even broke a train car's window. The camp police detectives were hot on our heels but they never caught us.

When our counselors weren't around, some of my friends and I would play a game we called chicken with a pocket knife. This involved two people standing face to face a few feet apart with their legs spread as wide as possible. They would then take turns throwing the knife between the other person's legs. If the knife stuck in the ground, the person whose legs it landed between would have to move one of their legs to the spot where the knife was sticking out of the ground. As the game progressed, the contestants' legs would get closer and closer together until the fear of losing a toe got to one of them and they would lose the game by "chickening out".

Sometimes, we were sent out to raise funds for different church causes from the faithful. I was a very good collector. I kept about half of the money for myself and still earned several trophies for being a top fund raiser. As a big city kid, small town kids looked up to me. I would tell them stories such as I was raised in a garbage can and then we moved to a cardboard box. They would listen in awe and believe me.

That summer I used a cigarette as a timer and igniter for a pack of firecrackers, putting them in a garbage can just below our living room window. Then I went up to watch TV with my Dad. Just when it seemed like too much time had passed and nothing would happen, BANG! BANG! BANG! BANG! BANG! My dad jumped out of his chair shaking his fist and yelling,"Those God Damn Kids!" He was really riled up and I got a really big kick out of it!

I started reading books like Abbie Hoffman's Steal This Book in addition to the underground newspapers. For those of you who don't know about Abbie Hoffman, he was a prominent counter culture activist, a founding member of the Yippies, and one of the Chicago Seven. They are most famous for their anti-war protests at the 1968 Democratic National Convention in Chicago, and being charged with conspiracy and inciting to riot at or near the convention. He also wrote other books such as "Revolution For The Hell Of It," "Fuck The System," "Woodstock Nation,"and "Steal This Urine Test." I was now becoming a real little hippie. On the ride home from church, there was usually a bearded long haired hippie on Wisconsin Avenue selling underground newspapers. He would call out, "Kaleidescope: take it home and read it folks."

When my mom took my sisters and me to Florida to visit her sister, I promptly went down to the local hardware store and bought 100 #14 brass washers and put scotch tape over the holes just like Steal This Book instructed. Then I used them to clean out the entire candy machine at the motel where we were staying.

Later that year, I took the few dollars I had and bought a one way Greyhound ticket to Chicago just for the adventure. When I got there, I was broke and didn't know what to do. A counter person called my folks and they had to wire money down for my return trip. I put the 25 cents I had left in a vending machine and got a miniature lighter. It was made of real metal and I still have it to this day, along with a real metal miniature pocket knife. You don't find those kinds of prizes anymore. A rabbit's foot to put on your key chain for good luck was also a popular prize back then.

Paperboy Pandemonium

That fall I started helping one of the guys in the neighborhood with his paper route on Sunday mornings. He was our paperboy and I had gotten to know him when my dad caught him and his friend pissing on my snow fort and tearing it down in the back yard. They got a tongue lashing, apologized, and everything was OK. We didn't want to lose our Journal delivery. Almost everyone subscribed to the local newspaper back then. He paid me $1.00 each Sunday morning which I promptly spent on a bowl of chicken noodle soup afterwards at the local restaurant where many of the neighborhood paperboys gathered after their routes.

A few months later I got my own gig with The Milwaukee Journal selling the Sunday edition on 27th and Wells from 4am-11am. In that period, I could sell 80 papers. The guys would come over to my corner after finishing their routes and we would pitch coins against the wall. Whoever was closest got to keep all of them each time we threw.

It was on this same corner that another paperboy and I climbed up the fire escape to the roof of a four story apartment building. We then laid down and took pot shots at passing cars, sniper style, with his BB rifle.

In less than a year, I had my own paper route. Three of my fellow paperboys and I became close friends. On Saturday nights we would meet up around 8pm and get a pizza at John's.

The oldest looking guy would go into a bar and get a six pack. We would cruise around drinking, go to the downtown YMCA and play pool, or go to the paper shack and play poker for quarters.

While at the "Y" one night, we spotted a middle aged guy who was really drunk. We decided to see if we could roll him and get his money. Following him upstairs, we made our approach as he was entering his room. He pulled a knife on us and we ran as fast as we could. That was the last time we tried anything like that.

One time, while cruising around, I was in the front passenger seat and decided to moon some people on the sidewalk in front of a country bar called Nick's Nickabob. The police pulled us over and said, "What was hanging out of the window?" I replied, "Just my hand, sir." Fortunately, he wasn't sure what he saw so they let us go. My friends had dumped their beer out through a hole in the floorboards.

At midnight, we'd turn off the lights at the paper shack and take a short nap on the benches. Around 2am, the main section of the newspaper would arrive. We assembled it with the other sections (called subbing) and were off to do our routes. We had some wild times at that shack. Once, the station captain picked me up and held me upside down and all the coins from my paper sales went flying everywhere. Another time my friends tied me to one of the metal benches and put it right under the heater. Then there was the time someone lit Lenny's hair on fire. He was not injured. He was the token black kid and always got the most ribbing even though he was completely accepted by us.

Apparently, I was a cute kid because I got solicited by some of the neighborhood pedophiles. When I came to collect for the newspaper delivery, one guy offered me $20.00 to come into his apartment for 20 minutes. I asked, "To do what?" He said, "Watch TV." That sounded too good to be true so I passed. When I got home, I told mom about it. She had her policeman friend check him out and, sure enough, he already had a sex conviction.

One of my friends was the 8th grade class president and after graduation we went behind the school to smoke a joint. Unfortunately, several of the younger kids followed us and we had to put off our first experience with marijuana.

At 14, I won a trip to Washington D.C. by selling the most new subscriptions to the Journal. I went with a group of other paper carriers and a few managers. I have no idea why, but I set a smoke bomb off in the elevator of The Ambassador Hotel where we were staying and it burned a hole in the nice wood trim. Two kids that were on the same elevator told on me but I denied it and, since they were black and I was white, just like the managers, the managers believed me. Upon returning, my paperboy friends gave me the nickname "Young Arse".

 That summer, my friend from the paper shack and I decided to go shoplifting at Target. We split up. I stole some small items, bought a bicycle tire patch kit and left the store to stash the items in my bicycle bag. Returning to buy a huge glazed donut I had seen after checking out, a man said "Jerry." When I looked at him, he walked up and said "Jerry, your friend Victor has just been arrested for shoplifting." The store detective said she saw me putting things in my pockets. I said "I put them back." They searched me and found nothing. The police came and took us to the police station. On the way there, they asked how we got to the store. My friend said, "bicycle" and I said, "The bus." When they asked, "Well which was it, bicycle or bus?" we both kept our mouths shut. My dad picked us up, we went back to the store to get our bikes and, none the wiser, he hauled all my stolen items home.

Jerry Runs Away From Home for Near A Year At Age 14
Still 14, I did not like the rules my parents were trying to impose on me. I had finished church grade school and they wanted me to go to the church high school. I wanted to go to public high school with my friends. They also wanted me to cut my long hair and quit my paper route because they felt the friends I met there were a bad influence on me. I was having none of it.

I had a grade school crush who had moved to Nevada and I decided to run away and go to Carson City, Nevada where she lived. I bought a plane ticket to Reno a month in advance and packed my records and books in a box mailing them general delivery to Carson City. I bought bags for my bicycle to store clothes and camping gear in and got a box from a bicycle shop to ship my bike in when I got to the airport. Having a few hundred dollars in savings from my paper route to take along left me in pretty good shape. I got up before anyone else on the day of my departure, snuck out of the house and, holding the large bicycle box with one arm, rode the 10 miles to the airport. There I disassembled my bike, put it in the box and checked it. I then called my mom and told her I was leaving but not where I was going.

When I arrived in Reno, I reassembled my bike and hit the road. It was already getting kind of late and the 30 mile ride through the mountains seemed like a bit much so I found a campsite a few miles down the road and tried to set up my tent. Alas, the soil was too hard to get the stakes in. Then I tried to light my sterno stove to make some food. Unfortunately, it was too windy. Tired, I just gave up, crawled into my unerected tent, and went to sleep,

The next day was rewarding with a long downhill ride into Carson City. While taking a break at a wayside, a man came up to me and said, "I've been on the road a long time and I can tell you are a runaway. There are a lot of drug dealers who hang out here and if you stay here you will get in with the wrong crowd. Here is the phone number of a lady that can help you out." I called the number and sure enough she found a place for me to stay for a few days and we called my parents. She then found a family that was willing to take me in. I stayed with them for five months going to Carson High School for the first semester of my freshman year.

It was there that I first heard "Stairway to Heaven" by Led Zeppelin. I would put a little AM radio under my pillow and listen before going to sleep. That evening, I was listening to a station from San Francisco and the famous Wolfman Jack was the DJ. He announced the song and, as it was playing, I had an epiphany, realizing that I was born a Rock and Roller. It doesn't get much better than that for a 14 year old.

Sometimes on weekend afternoons, the older son of the people I was staying with and a few other teenagers would drive one of the family pickup trucks to the hills around town and go four wheeling. Once, we ran right over a "No Trespassing" sign and were met at the end of the dirt road by a man in a pickup with a shotgun. We turned around and took off with everyone but the driver keeping their heads down. It was quite a chase! He finally caught up to us and made us come back and put his sign back up. Good country fun!

The Christians I was living with felt I was getting in with kids at school who were a bad influence on me, so they sent me off to a Christian boarding school near Watsonville, CA. It was right on the ocean and two of their sons were students there.

I liked California quite a bit. One Sunday while walking on the beach, my friend and I came across 20 people playing volleyball-all nude! In the dorm at school I used a trick I learned in "Steal This Book" by cutting a thin strip of cardboard and shoving it down the dime slot of the pay phone and then putting pennies in the nickel slot, I was able to make long distance calls at a 90% discount. The phone credited those pennies as if they were dimes! My friend and I also jimmied the door to the media room at school and played "Alice's Restaurant" in its entirety, piped to all the men's dorm rooms one Saturday night.

At the end of the school year, I was missing my family and friends and decided to return to Milwaukee. My parents gave me more of the freedom I required when I returned. I was now allowed to attend public school, get another paper route, and grow my hair long.

Back Home For More High School Havoc

Sophomore   Junior

I attended a technical high school for my sophomore year and started dealing pot. Those stories will be visited later in Wheeling and Dealing Daze. I also began skipping out of class on a regular basis. It was there that I learned that I was not well suited for auto repair since I was the only one in shop class who couldn't put a small engine back together.

The next year I transferred to a high school closer to home. There I got in with a crowd called "The Freaks." We were the pot smoking group. Other kids, like some of the "Jocks", got high too, but they were more secretive, not wanting to ruin their reputations. We didn't care. Some of the people in our group even got high before school. That was too early for me.

One time my mom got so tired of me sleeping in that she grabbed my arm and dragged me out of bed. It didn't do any good. As soon as she left my room, I locked the door and went back to sleep. I never arrived at school in time for homeroom and eventually they took me off the roll call list.

Once, when I was supposed to put on a record to accompany a film strip in class, I put on a Robin Trower record instead.

We would have quarter barrel parties at a place we called "Old Milwaukee." It was close to school, just across the freeway from County Stadium (Now Miller Park) under a huge electrical tower. My friend and I would climb up to the top of the tower and throw lit firecrackers down. I can still hear some of the girls screaming, "Jerry, come down!"

While on our lunch break, we would occasionally go to a local bar to have a few beers and play pool. They never carded us and they are still in business. I even went out to a downtown nightclub at 16, ordering a Tequila Sunrise instead of beer to appear older and more sophisticated.

At School that fall, I fell in love with Edith. She was such a cute little blond and very friendly to me. She invited me over to her house to play pool and smoke pot at lunch when her parents were at work. I fell hard for her, writing poems and doing everything possible to win her affection. Unfortunately, she only wanted to be friends. I tried to commit suicide twice, feeling I couldn't go on without her love. Once, I took a whole bottle of pills in the attic of my parent's house which I had fixed up as my party room. Somehow, after all those pills, I got up and promptly went crashing down the stairs. My mom called the paramedics. They took me to the hospital and pumped my stomach. A day later, I walked out without being discharged. I felt fine, so off I went.

"Old Milwaukee"

Some of my friends would come over to my folks' house to party. I would let a rope down from my bedroom window and they would tie a 12 pack to it. I hoisted it up and they came to the front door and had my parents let them in like nothing was going on. One of my friends had a purse big enough to put a 12 pack in! The old lady next door didn't like my friends and several times she yelled at some of the girls calling them "whores" and telling them, "Put some clothes on!" One time my mom came up to tell me I had a phone call and caught my friend with a bong pressed to his lips.

My paperboy friends and I also went out to several bars on a number of occasions sending "Red", who had lots of facial hair, up to order a pitcher of beer. The Landmark, and The Who's Inn (now Miss Katie's Diner) were our main haunts.

The Site, and later, The Alternate Site were on park land on Lake Michigan where local groups played for free during the summer for a mostly hippie type crowd. One time the police were harassing some of us and someone threw a bottle cutting a copper's head open. The next day there was a picture of it in the newspaper and I still have several copies to this day. The Milwaukee Police Chief, Harold Brier, was very anti hippie. I wore a pin that said "Retire Brier."

On my 16th birthday, my paper shack friends gave me two record albums: Bad Company- Bad Company, and Ringo Starr- Ringo. Those records along with Alice Cooper- Billion Dollar Babies, Arlo Guthrie- Alice's Restaurant, Chicago- Chicago, and Deep Purple-Made in Japan, were my first records. My collection would eventually grow to over 500.

My very first big rock concert was just one month after my 16th birthday. Deep Purple and ELO at the Arena. A local newspaper declared it, "long, loud." It was a strange combination of groups, but I enjoyed them both immensely and became a concert fanatic. I have attended hundreds of shows since.

Reliable Jerry

Through all of the wild times, I was a reliable worker. Never afraid of hard work, I started shoveling snow for our neighbors at age ten. Lots of snow. I even shoveled one multi-family building with a long driveway and large parking area. I loved making money. When I became a paperboy at age twelve, I was able to work my way up to larger and larger routes. At the peak of my paperboy career, I had a double route with eight apartment buildings and two hundred and fifty Sunday customers. Because I gave my customers excellent service, they rewarded me with great tips. Once, one of my customers complained about me. She claimed I had not delivered her paper for several days. I found out that someone had been stealing it. I was mad about her complaint and the next day she received her paper ripped in half. After that she apologized to me, started giving me a nice tip, and all was good.

Pesky Pedophiles

I missed my new friends in Nevada and California and, after my sophomore year, I bought a Greyhound Ameripass which gave me unlimited rides for 30 days. Heading west, the bus pulled into the station in Salt Lake City at 2am. Everybody had to get off for "cleaning." I still must have been a cute kid. While sitting in the station, a man came up to me and asked if I would like to come up to his apartment and watch a movie. The answer was no, of course.

When I returned to Milwaukee, I ran a classified ad in the newspaper looking for work. Since I already had quite a bit of experience with men approaching me for sex, I told people right up front that I was not interested in any gay business. A man hired me to help deliver lamps for his business. He assured me that there would be no funny business. The first day we were driving around in his van and he was telling me about his wife, family, and church. The next thing I knew he said, "Do you want a blow job?" I said, "I thought I said no gay business." He replied in a very forceful manner, "I'm not gay just a little bi" and proceeded to tell me that sometimes kids who work for him like to "get high" and then "get a blow job." I assured him I was not one of those and, fortunately, he did not force himself on me. Needless to say, that was the first and last day working for him.

Another time a guy approached me when I was walking in Juneau Park and said, "Some guys like the girls, some guys like the guys, me I swing either way." I replied, "Well you can swing away from me!"

My senior year of high school is pretty much a blur. It was one party after another. I paid the kid sitting next to me in chemistry so I could copy his work since I was not in class very often. I did not graduate from high school due to the frequent absences, but did get the few credits still needed a couple years later at Milwaukee Area Technical College.

At 17, I rented my first place with a friend. He was 18 so we qualified. It wasn't fancy, but we were able to party, crank the Rock and Roll, and have girls over. We furnished it by breaking into storage lockers on our paper routes and taking whatever we needed. It didn't last long. We got into a physical altercation and I moved back home.

Canoe Capers

At 19, my friend Rick and I went on a 9 day canoe trip on the Missinaibi River in Ontario, Canada with a group from my mom's church. Elder Mercer, who was a pastor from northern Wisconsin, was the group leader. The terrain was very wild and scenic. We saw Indians in canoes with shotguns and asked them what they were hunting. Surprisingly, it was fish. They set up nets to catch sturgeons that were 5-6 feet long and had to shoot them. Another Indian we met invited us back to his cabin to get high. Upon arrival, we found him in bed with squaws on both sides, playing Joan Baez on an 8 track player.

Pistol Packing Preacher

One night, during this trip, Rick and I were getting high in our tent when we heard our door being unzipped. The preacher poked his head in and pointed a large shiny revolver at us. He said, "Give me all your drugs or I am going to shoot you." I had the pot and Rick had some hash. I gave him my pot and we said that was all we had. Fortunately, he believed us and did not do any searching. What a scare! This was the first time anyone pulled a gun on me, but it would be far from the last! He must have snuck the gun into Canada, since most people are not allowed to possess handguns there. We were much more careful about where we got high after that.

The good preacher's son and another kid decided they were going to run a rapid called Hells Gate instead of doing a long portage. While we were carrying our canoe on the portage trail, they came walking out of the woods looking like they had seen a ghost. Barely escaping with their lives, their canoe and all of its contents were lost in the rapids.

Neither Rick nor I got lucky with the bubbly, busty, blond that we were both pursuing but one of the young ladies who was from northern Wisconsin invited me into the woods to show me "how they do it up in the north woods without getting poison ivy". That was a very educational experience!

The trip ended in Moosonee on the James Bay. We were able to find someone to buy us beer there since the drinking age in Canada was 21. We met some local Indians and invited them to join us across the river at our campsite for some partying that night. They arrived, promptly pushed their canoe out into the water, and it floated away. They told us that they had stolen it and didn't want to get caught. At the end of the night, we had to wake up the pastor to ferry them back to the mainland.

Mike The Maniac Millwright

One night I was out partying with crazy Mike. He was a millwright from West Virginia who was working with his dad on a project at the Oak Creek power plant. He stayed at my place that night. The next day I came home from work and he was gone, along with a lot of my belongings, including 300 vinyl records. I was able to reach him by phone and he sounded as surprised as I was. I then went around asking everyone in the building if they had seen anything. One guy had. He said he saw a couple of girls, who lived in the building

38

on my floor, carrying things out that day. I confronted them and told them that if I didn't get my things back in 24 hours I would call the police. It worked. I got almost everything back. When we came home drunk the night before, I had left my key in the door and one of them filched it.

I call Mike "Crazy Mike" because he liked to do a lot of crazy things. For instance, he loved renting muscle cars for the weekend, drinking a bunch of Jack Daniels, taking the car for a wild ride, beating the crap out of it, and then taking it to a chop shop where they would remove some good parts and replace them with damaged ones. He also loved chasing women, even though he had a wife back in West Virginia. One time he picked up three girls at Summerfest. One was good looking but her friends were not. She told him she would sleep with him if he slept with her girlfriends first. He did. When he left town, he asked me if I could put up his half- brother who had some "legal troubles" back home. I had never met him but reluctantly agreed. Mike gave me a few hundred dollars toward his rent.

The Evil Moron

When Jim arrived, I was totally shocked. Mike may have been kind of crazy but this guy was a total idiot…. Six feet four inches of pure evil. I got him a job where I worked and they nicknamed him, "The Evil Moron." When he drank, he would beat people up for no reason, sometimes jumping out of my car and attacking a complete stranger on the street. Jim met a friend of mine from high school at my apartment and they started sleeping together. My cooking oil went missing one day. I found the empty bottle in the living room where Jim had been shacking up with my friend. I don't even want to think about what they used all of it for. He never paid me any rent.

Soon thereafter, he was caught stealing at work, got fired, and moved back to West Virginia. Not long after his departure, referring to him, my friend who had been sleeping with him confided in me. She said, "Jerry, a 10" cock isn't everything."

Defective Foot

I enjoyed speeding and got quite a few tickets. I would always go to court and try to get them reduced to a lesser charge with fewer points. On one of these occasions, I appeared in front of Judge Panageos claiming I had a defective speedometer. He said, "Defective speedometer? I think you have a defective foot," but gave me a break anyway. He then said he wanted to see my driving record and noticed I had another defective equipment conviction. He shook his finger at me and said, "That's what I thought, I know about you guys."

That same year I was caught in a speed trap on my motorcycle in a small town in Minnesota. Since I was from another state, the police demanded that I follow them to the courthouse for a hearing, or post the fine as bond on the spot. I said I didn't have that much money with me. In court, the judge had the option of putting me in jail for the night or letting me return at a later date for court. He chose the latter, telling me that if I did not return, my license would be suspended in Minnesota. I never returned.

My Best Ride In A Police Car

At 21, I met a 16 year old girl while visiting some friends in Round Lake, Illinois. I took her on a motorcycle ride and she jumped me in the woods. No, I wasn't robbing the cradle. She had already had an abortion. She lived in Wisconsin Dells and we became a long distance couple. One weekend I came up to visit. She said she wanted to come back to Milwaukee with me and that it was OK with her folks. The next day there was a knock on my apartment door. It was two detectives from The Milwaukee Police Department looking for Cheryl. Apparently, she had not told her folks about the trip and, at some point, they had written my license plate number down. When they asked if I had seen Cheryl, I said, "Yes, she is right here." They took us downtown to the station and called her folks. She spoke with them and then put me on the line. I assured them that I would bring her home the next day. After the call, the detectives took us both back to my apartment and dropped us off. Things were a little different back then!

Black Sabbath Riot At The Milwaukee Arena 10-9-80

This tour was billed as "The Black and Blue Tour" and it sure lived up to its name. Blue Oyster Cult came on first. They put on a long and exciting set with lasers and great lighting effects. I was getting a little worried because by the time they left the stage it was after 10pm and I had heard that by law the show had to be over by 11pm.

Black Sabbath came on shortly before 11pm and walked off stage during their second song. Nothing happened for 10 minutes. Then their stage manager came out and started yelling at the crowd. He said someone had thrown a bottle and hit Geezer, their bass player, in the head and they wouldn't be playing anymore. That's when all hell broke loose. I was sitting about half way up. People started breaking off their seats and throwing them toward the stage. Others flooded onto the main floor and piled all the chairs up in one big pile. Then someone tried to set them on fire. Just then a large group of cops came rushing onto the floor and began clubbing people. They made an announcement that anyone who didn't leave would be arrested. I headed up to the nearest hallway to exit. People were throwing cigarette and candy vending machines out of the windows and chanting "fuck the cops."

Outside, concert goers were jumping on the parked cop cars and breaking the windows. Eventually, the cops closed off the entire street and forced everyone to leave. If someone had thrown a bottle, they would have been severely punished by the crowd. Afterwards, it was revealed that the bottle had actually fallen from above. It was, presumably, accidentally knocked over by a member of the lighting crew. If Geezer was really injured, he made a full recovery.

Motorcycle Madness
At 22, I took a motorcycle trip to St. Louis, Denver, and The Pine Ridge Indian Reservation in South Dakota on my Yamaha RD350 motorcycle with my friend Cheryl who is 50% Native American. We attended the First Annual VP Fair in St Louis at Jefferson National Expansion Memorial on the Fourth of July and saw Pure Prairie League. You had better watch yourself while crossing the street around there because they stop for no one. We did meet some very hospitable folks who put us up for the night.

Upon arriving in Colorado, we headed for Pikes Peak. My motorcycle died half way up. I turned around, coasted downhill, popped the clutch, and, boom, the engine started. I turned around again and made it all the way to the top. This was the first time I had ever been on top of a 14,000 ft. mountain. That night we bought a 6 pack at a gas station. After a few beers, I did not feel a thing. It was then that I noticed the printing on top of the can that said 3.2 (weak) beer. I still have

a full unopened can that is now over 35 years old! On to Red
Rocks where we saw The Marshall Tucker Band. A lot of
people brought in their own food and it seemed like half the
people around us were eating fried chicken!

Our last stop was The Pine Ridge Indian Reservation. I had
never seen such poverty before. There were no phones and the
house was heated with a wood burner. There was garbage all
over outside and the skinniest dogs I have ever seen running
around. Cheryl told me not to let any of her relatives drive my
motorcycle because if they did it would not be in good enough
condition to drive back home.

We drove over 2500 miles on that trip. I took a RD350 around
the block a few years ago and my hands were tingling so badly

from the vibrations that I could barely hold on. We also had all of our personal and camping gear loaded on the back of that little motorcycle.

Beer Delivering and Hell Raising

When I returned from Colorado, I got a job delivering beer for a beer distributor. One of the guys I met there and his friends threw a big party in the Kettle Moraine State Forest in the middle of winter. They called it "The Adirondacks party." We hiked to a three sided shelter, built a fire and mixed up a big batch of "Whopatooli"- a mixture of all kinds of booze and maybe a little soda or juice. We had a roaring fire and every time no one was watching, someone would throw a glass of gas on and it would really flare up. I took some acid, drank lots of that devilish concoction and ended up passing out and rolling down a hill in the snow. No one bothered to check on me so I was very lucky to wake up a few hours later without any injuries.

Get A Real Bike

Noticing that many of the bars we delivered to had basements full of empty half barrels, which had no deposit in those days, I did some research and found a salvage dealer willing to pay me $3.00 for each stainless steel barrel and $4.00 for each aluminum barrel. My employer had three delivery trucks and crews. I bought an old C-20 ambulance type truck for $60.00 and painted all the windows except the windshield so no one could see inside. The passenger door on the truck did not latch well. You should have seen the looks on my friends' faces when we took a right turn and their door went flying open! I parked a block away from work each day and told the other delivery crews that I had a friend who was making grills out of the barrels and they would be paid 50cents each for every one deposited in my truck. My boss didn't care because he wasn't making anything for handling the barrels.

The reason there were so many empties in the bars was that the brewery delivery drivers were too lazy to remove them when they delivered new barrels. They preferred sitting in the bar and having a beer which was allowed back then. Several bars even bought me a drink for getting the barrels out of their way!

Each morning on the way to work I would stop at the salvage dealer, unload my haul, and get paid $50.00-100.00. My goal was to save enough to buy my dream motorcycle, a brand new 1981 Honda 750 Custom in Blue. After the Brady Street Festival, one of the workers spotted over 100 barrels in Giovani's Restaurant parking lot and promptly hauled them to his backyard a few blocks away. That was a windfall!

At one point I thought I could get even more for them since some of the nearby counties had a $10.00 deposit. Once, I had my parents' single car garage full to the ceiling. I was able to make one trip and get $10.00 for each barrel but after that they would not take them.

One day a Schlitz executive saw my salvage dealer hauling a truck load of barrels and came to visit the dealer's place of business. He told him that the barrels were the property of the breweries and if he was caught with them again they would press charges. That was the end of the golden goose but not before enough money was made to get my new motorcycle. I even had enough for all the extra bells and whistles like an alarm system, radar detector, fairing with adjustable windshield , adjustable back rest, radio, cassette player, and cruise control.

My First Claim To Fame

My friend Cheryl and I attended Summerfest together on June 30, 1982. I made a hat from a beer tray and put one empty beer cup in each of the four corner drink holders. People went wild when they saw it giving me high fives and taking my picture. Then a newspaper reporter saw me and took a picture.

It appeared in the paper the very next day and became the first time I had fifteen minutes of fame. I still break out that hat for Summerfest occasionally and it is always a big hit.

Young, Wild, and Free To Roam

In early July, I quit my job, hopped on my new bike and headed west. I was 23 and had the world by the balls. I had money in my pocket, no time line, and nothing but fun and adventure ahead. My first stop was in western Wisconsin to visit some friends and relatives.

On to Minnesota where I met a charming young lady while having a small repair done at an electronics store. Then, it was off to The Black Hills of South Dakota. Have you dug Wall Drug? I have! I met another motorcyclist while entering a campground in the Black Hills. We agreed to split the cost of a campsite and ended up finding out that we both went to the same high school and lived close to each other in Milwaukee.

The next day we went swimming in one of the fabulous lakes nearby. There we met another motorcyclist who had a bike exactly like mine. Dave was from Lacrosse, WI. We all had our motorcycles custom painted in the Black Hills by "The Lightning Painter". See picture at bangheader.com Go to
 the pictures link and enter code bangheaderspics
The three of us traveled together for three weeks.

Our next stop was Yellowstone National Park and The Grand Tetons nearby. It was really fun riding with some like- minded free spirits. We hiked and cruised all over the parks seeing large herds of animals, the thermal area, Yellowstone Lake, Mammoth Hot Springs, and The Grand Canyon of the Yellowstone. Onward to Glacier National Park, where Dave and I went rafting on the north fork of the Flathead River in the inflatable raft I brought on the back of my cycle.

"Going To The Sun" Road In Glacier National Park

The river was a little wilder than we expected and we ended up under water! We lost a paddle and several shoes. Fortunately, we found another paddle downriver. It was very interesting driving my cycle the 45 miles back to the campground with no shoes. We did come across a bar in the middle of nowhere on the way. I drank a couple of Blind Russians and warmed up.

After Glacier, my new friends headed back and I was on my own. The next stop was Olympic National Park in Washington and then Crater Lake in Oregon. The seashore in Oregon is so rugged and wild, it almost feels like you are in another world.

When I pulled into Eureka, California, some people really got a kick out of the wooden canoe paddle strapped vertically to my backrest and immediately befriended me. Soon we were headed to the bar for a few drinks. They invited me back to their apartment to partake in some sweet leaf. Humboldt County bud sure lives up to its reputation. They were passing joint after joint around but all I needed was a few puffs. More wasted than ever before! Wow that was the real deal! They asked me where I was heading and I said, "LA." They were shocked and wondered why I would want to go to a place like that.

The Redwoods, San Francisco and Yosemite National Park were my next stops. My friend, Cheryl now lived and worked in Yosemite and she took me on some great hikes and rides!

Heading south to Carson City, I visited the family I lived with when I ran away at 14, and nearby Lake Tahoe which is one of the most gorgeous lakes I have ever seen.

Back to the coast on Hwy 1. This is one of the most scenic drives I have ever been on... Big Sur, Santa Cruz with its Boardwalk, The Monterey Bay, Santa Barbara and everything in between. Just spectacular!

Arriving in LA, I decided to visit the famous Hollywood Boulevard. I went to a motel and asked how much their rooms were for a night. The clerk said, "We don't rent rooms by the night, only by the hour." I thought to myself, they must have some fast sleepers around here. While still on Hollywood Blvd., I stopped for dinner a few blocks down. I sat at the counter and ordered a chicken dinner. Just after it arrived a man sat down right next to me. The next thing I knew a hand was reaching for my plate and he grabbed a piece of chicken! The manager threw him out and replaced my missing breast!

I got in touch with my high school friend Edith who had moved to LA. We went to all of the great beaches including Venice Beach where, on any given day, you can see...well, what can't you see would be more accurate. We also attended the US concert (pronounced us as in excuse us).

The US Concerts- 1982 and 1983

I was just 10 years old when the Woodstock concert was held. Unfortunately, my parents were not hippies and we did not attend. The closest I have ever come to that moment in rock history was the US concerts. They were sponsored by Steve Wozniak, also known as "Woz", who is one of the founders of Apple Computers. Just 13 and 14 years after Woodstock, I was now old enough to make it there on my own! I was on my 11 week motorcycle trip out west when I attended the 1982 show.

Leaving my bike at Edith's place, we took her car to the Glen Helen Regional Park 60 miles east of LA in the desert. It was quite a hike from the parking lot to the concert site and the temperature was 100 degrees plus. We found a drinking fountain on the way but it didn't work. I twisted the head off and a continuous stream of water shot up in the air. Many concert goers gratefully ran under the cooling water.

When we arrived at the concert site, I saw several people holding up signs that said, "LSD For Sale." I bought some and proceeded to enjoy the music. The Police were the first evening's headliner. When they started jamming, I surged toward the stage and lost Edith. After the show, it was getting cold so I covered myself with a couple of tee shirts I had bought and some sage brush and tried to sleep.

1983 US Concert

The next day I got smart. A lot of people came out from LA for the day, spreading blankets on the grass. As the day went on they got wasted and wandered off. That's when I moved in and got myself a blanket. The next two nights were nice and warm! A lot of the ladies were watching the show topless.

On the last day I met a lady and we hit it off right away. We ended up having sex in her sleeping bag while one of the groups was playing. A cop went right by us on horseback while we were doing it. We were so hot for each other that we did it again in the parking lot before saying our goodbyes. I also met a beer vendor who was willing to trade beer for pot. That worked out really well since the beer was quite expensive.

In 1983, I decided to convert a small school bus into a party bus and drive it to the concert. I advertised in The Milwaukee Journal as "Party Bus to US" and put one way mirrored coverings on all of the windows. Unfortunately, I did not get many responses and the bus had some mechanical problems prior to the trip so I decided to ride with a friend who was moving to California.

His car broke down in North Platte, NE. The shop said it looked pretty bad and we should get a room. When we checked back later, his engine was hanging from a chain on the back of a tow truck. Instead of replacing it, my friend wanted it rebuilt. That took three days. He just wanted to stay in the room and smoke cigarettes. I went to a bar and met a lady who took me home. In the morning, she gave me a tee shirt that said, "If You Ain't A Nebraska Cowboy You Ain't Shit."

We still made it to California in time for the concert. This time I had a small tent and sleeping bag. We set up camp in the parking lot. About 12:30am a Mexican guy came around with hot homemade tamales for sale. They were cheap and delicious. What a treat in the middle of the night.

At the concert grounds there were huge video screens on both sides of the stage to accommodate over 100,000 people who were in attendance each day. A total of 670,000 people attended that weekend making it the 5th biggest concert in the world's history, even bigger than Woodstock. There was a large shower area with many shower heads but no shower curtains so everyone was just showering out in the open naked! During the heat of the day, there were huge water cannons that were used to spray the crowd down, cooling us off.

I attended both years for all three days. It was rumored that all of the headlining groups in 1983 were paid one million dollars apiece.

The musical lineup for both years was awesome. The second day of the '83 show had an amazing lineup with my favorite metal bands. There were over 300,000 people there that day and I have never seen so many headbangers in one place, before or since. Everyone was friendly and peaceful. Drugs, Sex, and Rock N Roll were plentiful. I don't know how much closer to Woodstock you can get than that.

After the show I held up a sign that said, "I need a ride to Chicago." Three young people agreed to let me join them. We shared the cost of gas and driving duties and made it back to Chicago in 48 hours. Two hours on a bus and I was back home.

US Concert Lineup

Friday, September 3, 1982
The Police
The Ramones
The Talking Heads
The B-52s
The English Beat
Gang of Four
Oingo Boingo

Saturday, September 4, 1982
Tom Petty
Pat Benatar
The Kinks
Santana
The Cars
Dave Edmunds
Eddie Money

Sunday, September 5, 1982
Fleetwood Mac
Jackson Browne
Jimmy Buffet
Jerry Jeff Walker
The Grateful Dead
Hoyt Axton

Saturday, May 28, 1983
The Clash
Men At Work
Stray Cats
The English Beat
Flock of Seagulls
Oingo Boingo
Divinyls
Inxs

Sunday, May 29, 1983
Van Halen
The Scorpions
Triumph
Judas Priest
Ozzy Osbourne
Mötley Crüe
Quiet Riot

Monday, May 30, 1983
David Bowie
The Pretenders
Stevie Nicks
Missing Persons
U2
Joe Walsh
Quarter Flash
Berlin

In the summer of 1983, Pabst brewery workers went on strike during Summerfest. The beer distributor I used to work for was hired by Pabst to get Pabst beer into the Summerfest grounds. They hired me and my US bus for one day. We filled the bus from top to bottom with cases of Pabst and I drove it right past the picket lines. With the mirrored windows, nobody was the wiser.

Back to the '82 cycle trip. A friend of mine from high school had a brother living in LA and he and his roommates put me up for a week in the penthouse they rented on the corner of Wilshire and Western. Edith, her girlfriend, and I took a ride to Tijuana, Mexico one night in her car. We were drinking Seven and Sevens all the way down and, once we found a motel that didn't require us to give them our car keys, we checked in and I passed out. I woke up in the middle of the night dying of thirst and took a big drink from the water vase near my bed. Big mistake! The next day I was sick as a dog. We went out for breakfast and I ate a pepper from the jar on the table. Big mistake #2! Spent the next who knows how long outside trying to get right with the world. I felt like a mule had kicked me in the head for the next two days.

Edith had a friend in San Diego who we visited for a weekend. They have some great beaches there. Someone had brought some snow down from the mountains and made a snowman on the beach. I thought it was really cool and so "California" to see many people cruising along the beach on their bicycles in the late afternoon with a beer in their drink holder.

Hwy1 was so scenic that I did it again on my way back to Wisconsin. 11 weeks, 13,000 miles and spending quality time with eight different women. What a trip! I really did have the world by the balls.

Sexcapades 1978-1982 (ages 19-23)

This is not fifty shades of anything so you will be spared all graphic details. None of my canoeing BJ stories will be mentioned.

I have been a lucky man when it comes to women. I guess being tall, dark and some say handsome, a smooth talker, owning a nice motorcycle and usually having some good pot did not hurt. Having a fun, friendly, and outgoing personality helped too.

In my younger days, I guess you could call me a pussy hound because I pursued every possible opportunity to have sex. Things were different then. I had never heard of AIDS and, as far as my partners and I were concerned, it was an era of worry free sex.

Twice I had a chance to have a threesome and was fooling around with two ladies at once. Both times the lady I had been dating chickened out and I ended up having sex with her girlfriend. The second time my girlfriend had agreed to it and said, "You two go in the bedroom and get started and I will be right in." She never showed up!

At 20, I was leaving a bar at closing time. A young lady, who I had met there that evening, was standing on the sidewalk arguing with her boyfriend. I said, "You don't need this," picked her up and carried her away. Fortunately, she only lived a block away and had no objections to me removing her from that situation. Back at her place we had great sex all night long.

When I was 21, I worked selling furniture. I sold a lady a pit group. She invited me over and we had sex on her new pit group that night. I also brought several ladies into the furniture store and had sex with them on the beds in the showroom after business hours that same year.

On my eleven week motorcycle trip out west at age 23, I had sex with eight different women. Soon after departing, I had trouble with my stereo and stopped at an electronics store. A young lady I met working there was very friendly and attractive so I asked her out. She said she had to study. I left my cycle there for the repair and went shopping. Returning near closing time, I brought her some flowers and a bottle of wine. We sat in her car drinking the wine and talking for hours. She said she was staying at her brother's house and he was away so I could stay in the spare bedroom. When I came out of the bathroom, she was standing there naked. We had a great night, and the next morning as I was leaving, her "date" came to pick her up!

Another great time on this trip was had in Yellowstone National Park in the boiling river. Now the area is monitored by electronic gates and cameras, but back then, at night after the tourists left, it was open debauchery. In hot water a man can last a long time and the lady I met from Germany and I had quite the time.

On the same trip I visited the family I had lived with when I ran away from home at age 14. Their daughter who was just nine years old when I lived with them had grown up and was now eighteen. We were instantly attracted to each other and ended up making out the first night of my visit after her folks went to bed. The next day she and I went to Lake Tahoe on my motorcycle. Finding a secluded spot on a big rock on the east side of the lake, we got naked and enjoyed the afternoon swimming and I'll leave the rest up to your imagination. She wanted me to teach her how to smoke pot and I obliged.

Twice I had sex with different women while taking Quaaludes, sometimes referred to as "Ludes." They are no longer available, but back then they were a prescription anti-psychotic medication that released all inhibitions, greatly

59

increased body sensations and made me feel like Superman. Once I did them with an old friend from high school. We were at a bar and she said, "Jerry, I'm going to take you home and fuck your brains out." She wasn't lying. The other time, another lady friend and I took Ludes at a nature center next to a park on Lake Michigan. We were getting pretty frisky when an employee came up and said, "We will be closing in a few minutes and we are going to have to ask you to leave." No problem. We moved it to a secluded area of the park next door and went at it.

Once, while having sex at Devils Lake State Park, a group of people hiked past us on a trail just a few feet away. I have also had sex on the marker at The Cumberland Gap National Park and in four states at once at Four Corners.

While having sex at a motel, the headboard fell off of the wall and almost clocked me in the head. At another motel we were fooling around in the shower and water started leaking down to the room below. That's when the manager called!

I was watching a football game with a lady I had been dating for about a month. Out of nowhere she exclaimed, "If the Packers get a touchdown, you get a blow job!"

While canoeing on the Wisconsin River in Spring Green, WI., I met a young lady who was working the door at a class reunion which my friend and I ended up crashing. We walked into the restaurant/ hotel and she was handing out name tags. She knew several people who would not be in attendance and thought it would be funny to put their name tags on my friend and me. We really hit it off and somehow ended up having sex in the hotel's indoor hot tub at midnight before going back to her place and going at it all night. My canoeing buddy was a little pissed when I didn't return to our campsite until noon the next day.

Audacious Octoberfest

That fall I traveled to La Crosse, WI to visit my new friend Dave and check out their famous Oktoberfest. Talk about a drunk fest! There were people throwing beer up in the air all over and crawling on all fours to cross the street.

On October 10, 1982, the Milwaukee Brewers won the American League Championship and Milwaukee went wild. Milwaukeeans packed Wisconsin Avenue from east to west. I took a quarter barrel of beer downtown and let people drink straight from the tap. One guy climbed the flagpole in front of the library in his underwear!

More Fallout

That same fall I was riding my motorcycle and a guy pulled up next to me on his bike at a stop light on 27th and State St. When the light changed, he revved up his engine and took off. The next thing I knew, he was half a block ahead of me standing on the seat of his bike. I had a feeling that nothing good could come out of this so I stayed well behind him. After about 10 seconds of standing on his seat, he and his bike crashed into some parked cars. I didn't see any blood, but he was holding his helmet-less head and the paramedics were called.

Southern Surprises

I hooked up with my friend's sister and was in a committed relationship for five years soon after returning from the US concert in the summer of 1983. That fall she and I took a motorcycle trip to Kentucky, Tennessee, North Carolina, and West Virginia. A large part of the south that we saw was totally different than anything I was used to in Wisconsin or had seen out west.

The first night we stayed at Mammoth Cave National Park. I asked a park ranger where the nearest place to get a six pack of beer was. He informed us that we were in a dry county and the closest place to buy alcohol was in Bowling Green, 40 miles away.

Our next stop was Jellico, TN, which is on I-75 right on the Kentucky-Tennessee border. We stopped at a bar across the road from our motel for a beer and a game of pool. Three hillbillies approached us and insisted we play pool with them. Southern hospitality they called it. When the bar closed around 8pm, they invited us to, "Come see how us poor hillbillies live" and offered to let us try some of their moonshine. They said my girlfriend could ride with them in their car and I could follow on my motorcycle. Somehow, this did not seem like a situation that anything good would come out of. Just then, I had a vision of being tied to a tree and forced to watch their granddaddy rape my girlfriend. We politely declined their generous offer.

We traveled off of the interstate on some U.S. and State Highways through rural Kentucky. Many people had everything they ever owned that didn't work anymore piled up right in front of their house. We also saw many folks burning their garbage in 55 gallon drums next to the road.

In parts of North Carolina, you could not get alcoholic drinks at restaurants, but you could bring in your own liquor if it was in a brown bag, and kept out of sight on the floor. They would sell you juice or soda and give you a glass with ice to mix your own.

In West Virginia, you were not allowed to pump your own gas. All of the gas stations were full service. A couple of moonshiners we met told us about being chased through the mountain back roads by federal tax agents or "revenuers" as they called them. There were shots exchanged by both parties. One of the "Moonshiners" had a limp and used a cane claiming the "revenuers" had shot him. He had a back country doctor patch him up after they lost the revenuers.

In the North, most protestant religions allow you to go out to the bar on Friday or Saturday night and still go to church on Sunday. In the South, the line in the sand was much more pronounced. You are either a sinner who drinks or a God fearing person who goes to church. There is no in between... at least not in many rural areas.

They Are Great Smokey Mountains

One of the most memorable stops on the trip was The Great Smokey Mountain National Park. It is the most visited national park in the country for good reason. Not only is it in close proximity to many major cities, but it boasts the highest point in Tennessee, Clingmans Dome. Its summit can be reached on foot with a short but steep half mile hike from the parking lot.

We were rewarded at the summit with a nice tower offering a 360 degree view.

There is also a lodge on top of Mt. LeConte where you can stay overnight in the park. Their accommodations include all meals and great views. With five different trails available to reach the summit and several very nice waterfalls on the way, it is sheer paradise. See pictures at bangheader.com Go to the pictures link and enter code bangheaderspics

There are many other natural attractions to explore in the park and a good chance that you even may see a bear like I have on numerous occasions. Two of the most popular places to stay while visiting the park are Pigeon Forge and Gatlinburg. Both offer a huge variety of lodging. Gatlinburg is just north of the park and their accommodations are a bit pricier. That is not the only difference between the two towns. Just eight miles to the north is Pigeon Forge. To this day, you cannot buy hard liquor at a bar or liquor store there. Even though they are in the same county, you must go 8 miles down the road to Gatlinburg if you want the good stuff.

The American Rock Festival- 5-27-84 – Kalamazoo, MI

Two friends and I decided that this would be a great concert to attend. Quite a few of our favorite groups, including Mötley Crüe, Quiet Riot, Ratt, Accept, Ozzy Osborne and Triumph were scheduled to appear. It was an outdoor show being put on at Timber Ridge ski area. We chose to drive the 245 miles in our friend Steve's car.

Unfortunately, the car broke down in Michigan City, Indiana. We were determined to get to the show, which started the next day, so we negotiated with a cab company to take us the remaining 91 miles. Longest cab ride I had ever had! After 20 minutes, we asked the driver if we could drink our beer. He replied, "No problem." Twenty minutes later we asked, "Do you mind if we light up a joint?" He replied, "No problem, as long as you share it with me." Then we ran into a carload of ladies presumably heading to the same show and ended up having a friendly shouting match between vehicles for part of the trip. Arriving around 11pm, we learned that a car show was also in town and all the hotels were full. After spending over an hour searching for a room, we ended up putting our tent up in back of the Red Roof Inn.

The next morning, we found a better place to sleep after the show. We rented a U-Haul trailer that was in a gas station parking lot and stashed our camping gear in it for the day. When we returned that evening, we rolled out our sleeping bags and slept inside.

The show was awesome and the LSD I took enhanced the awe quite a bit. We were down in the main area for the earlier groups including OZZY. Vince Neil climbed 80ft. up on the scaffolding. That was quite a sight. The final group to play was Triumph. We climbed up on the hill and took in the whole spectacle. Over 50,000 people attended the show. The next day, still a little fuzzy, we boarded a Greyhound bus back to Milwaukee.

Mole Lake Blue Grass Festival- August 1-4, 1985

I attended this concert with several friends. It was held on an Indian reservation in northern Wisconsin. One of the highlights was the large circular tubs of drinks they sold with a cover and straws in six spots. It was a potent concoction they called "Combat Juice." The bonfires were huge, made with whole trees. The music was outstanding. At 2am, John Hartford was on stage playing "Hey Babe You Wanna Boogie?" I was drunk and lost my friends, who had a cabin a few miles down the road. I ended up passing out in the camping area on the ground. When I woke up in the morning, there were people lobbing little stones at me yelling, "Incoming!" That festival was one of the wildest I have ever attended.

More Amazing Concerts

I cannot remember all of the concerts I have attended nor will I bore you with all of the minute details of all the ones I can. These are just a few of the more memorable shows which I have not shared with you already.

OZZY

I have now seen Ozzy in 5 states, which is two more states than any other artist, and he always put on a helluva headbanging show. The first time was on January 22, 1982 in Milwaukee. I went to this show with "Jr." He was a Puerto Rican guy I worked with. I had one shot of the Puerto Rican moonshine he brought and was completely drunk for the entire concert! This show was just two days after he bit the head off of a bat at a concert in Des Moines, IA.

Some friends and I rented a Limo to go see Ozzy in Madison in 1983. My dealer, Scott, lit up a crack pipe in the limo. Excepting his girlfriend, no one else partook. Shortly after arriving at the venue, all of my friends ditched me because one of them wanted to go to the beer stand instead of meeting at the spot we had agreed on. It was a general admission show with no assigned seats so I ended up watching the show by myself. Afterwards I almost missed my ride home because I came out of the wrong side of the venue and couldn't find the limo for half an hour. When we needed to take a leak on the way home the driver pulled over on the freeway, got out, and opened the door for us!

At the Rosemont Horizon in Chicago, a guy in the next row lit up a crack pipe in front of us. The ushers didn't bother anyone unless they were in the wrong seat. At the same venue, a number of years, later Ozzy came across the rafters in a sleigh and was lowered down onto the stage. That tour was originally going to be called the "Black Christmas" tour, but since 9/11 had just occurred a few months earlier they changed the name to the "Merry Mayhem" tour.

Ozzfest at "The Gorge" in the state of Washington on August 27, 2002, a beautiful outdoor venue. I got crazy jumping around while System of a Down was playing. You had to drink your beer in "The Beer Garden," leave, and go through the line again if you wanted to have another one. No beer was allowed out of the beer garden. Ozzy was quite emotional when he asked everyone to pray for his wife, Sharon, who was fighting cancer.

Black Sabbath

Black Sabbath at the old Chicago Stadium (indoors). When we walked in, there was the largest cloud of pot smoke that I had ever seen filling the entire room!

Masters Of Metal-August 19, 2008, Tinley Park, IL Motorhead, Judas Priest, and Black Sabbath with DIO. Black Sabbath was billing themselves as "Heaven and Hell". This was the last time I saw DIO before his death and one of the last shows he ever played. They performed a lot of songs from their "Heaven and Hell" album, which I missed seeing on the original tour in Milwaukee due to Geezer being injured, and the band walking off stage during their second song, as described in "Black Sabbath Riot." With this show, everything came full circle for me.

The Rolling Stones

The Rolling Stones are another group that I have seen many times. They always put on a fantastic show and take elaborate staging to a whole new level. Once, when an interviewer asked Mick Jagger how they felt about all of their elaborate staging and lighting effects he said, "As long as the spectacle does not exceed the music it's alright with us." I concur. On their "Steel Wheels" tour at Alpine Valley there had been a lot of rain and people were sliding all the way down the big hill on the grass and getting completely covered in mud. Giant inflatable ladies were palpating up and down on both sides of the stage.

Cheap Trick

Cheap Trick at the Walworth County Fair. When I asked where the beer tent was they said, "This is a junior fair. We don't serve beer here." Good thing I brought my flask! In the same county, at a much larger outdoor concert venue called Alpine Valley, undercover cops sit on top of a van with jumper cables next to them at the first stop sign after you get off of the freeway. When you stop, they look into your car and observe any illicit smells. If they see any illegal open beverages or smell marijuana, they push a button on their walkie talkie which is hidden on their side. After you turn, the corner a marked police car pulls out of a farmhouse driveway and pulls you over. Of course they don't want to ruin your good time so, in most cases, they take you to their makeshift kangaroo court nearby and give you the option of paying a large fine or posting a large bail if you want, or come back to their small town court and fight the charges. It's all about getting your money. Just 40 miles from downtown Milwaukee, it is a whole different world. I always ask them if they need a jump! Their response is, "We've got someone on the way already." If you can get past their gauntlet, it is a great place to see a show.

Sir Paul McCartney

The Beatles were a great band. Unfortunately, I was only five when they played Milwaukee. A lot of their music was greatly overplayed on the radio, and my turntable and I grew tired of it. Paul is a different story, and ever since the Beatles broke up I have been a huge fan. When my friend's older brother got tickets to see the "Wings Over America" tour in Chicago on June 2, 1976, I was very envious, jealous, and disappointed that I could not attend.

The next time he toured in the US I was not going to be denied. By the time word of the show to be held in Chicago on December 3, 1989 reached me, only obstructed view tickets were available. I bought them. Hoping I could find better tickets at the venue, I arrived early on the day of the show. As I was walking around the venue a ticket window popped open. I dashed over and was the second person in line. Score! I got two tickets just off the floor straight back from the stage on the risers. That was a fantastic show! Since then I have been lucky enough to see Paul 5 more times at 5 different venues in Milwaukee and Chicago.

The last time I saw him perform in Milwaukee was on July 16, 2013 at Miller Park and what a show it was! He performed for almost two and a half hours with the temperature hovering around 90 degrees. Amazing! Paul, if you are reading this, the only unfulfilled rock and roll fantasy I have is you doing a tour playing only your post-Beatles songs. You have so many gems that we have yet to hear live. Alright, play some underplayed Beatles songs for the encore!

Pink Floyd

At the Pink Floyd "Animals" tour at the Milwaukee County Stadium on June 15, 1977, a giant inflatable pig was flying high over the stadium during the show. Out of the blue it blew up with a very loud bang. I still have my ticket stub. $9.00 for a ticket with a field pass. Phenomenal show.

The Who

Milwaukee was not originally one of The Who's tour stops on their farewell tour but Milwaukeeans gathered over 70,000 signatures in a petition drive, and "Tim the Rock N Roll Animal", who was a DJ at radio station WQFM, camped on the rooftop of the station. He would not come down until the group agreed to play Milwaukee. After 15 days, Roger Daltry's voice was heard on the radio promising the group would play here on December 7, 1982. Our arena was the smallest on their tour with just 11,700 seats. Over forty thousand orders were placed for tickets and I was fortunate enough to get two. One of my best all time concerts.

The Smashing Pumpkins

The Smashing Pumpkins at The Bradley Center on October 1, 1996 was a, well, shall I say "smashing" show. It was a Tuesday evening and the band left the stage after completing their set. That's when about half of the 18,000+ crowd got up and left. When the band returned to the stage for the first of what would become three encores their lead singer, Billy Corgan proclaimed, "Now that all the assholes who just came to hear our radio shit left, we're going to play some real music." They played on for about an hour.

Stone Temple Pilots

At The Bradley Center on December 13, 1996, I almost got caught up in a huge mosh pit. This was a very high energy concert and I was jumping up and down almost constantly like no other show before or since. Many stray shoes were left behind on the floor when the show was over.

Tom Petty

Tom Petty at Summerfest was the best smelling concert I have ever attended, especially when they played "Let's Roll Another Joint".

KISS and Judas Priest At The Milwaukee Arena 9-24-79

KISS had one of the most amazing stage setups I had ever seen and the largest number of trucks by far. 11 semi trucks full of equipment and the stage. The stage had pathways where the group could go on and off stage seamlessly. There was a lot of fire and a drum kit that rose high into the air. This was the first time I saw Judas Priest. They would become one of my favorite groups. I have now seen them at least 15 times in three states, and they always put on a great show. It is a rare

71

occasion when Rob Halford doesn't drive a Harley out on stage just before they play Hell Bent for Leather. This was my first headbanging show, and when you're a headbanger, it's not a huge leap to become a Bangheader!

<u>Led Zeppelin</u>

Led Zeppelin has always been one of my favorite bands, so when they announced four dates in Chicago for their fall 1980 tour, I jumped to get tickets. Ordering as many as I could, I got a total of 24. The plan was to sell all of the extra tickets and make a killing. Unfortunately, their drummer John Bonham died shortly before the tour was to begin, and it was canceled.

All was not lost. Their lead singer, Robert Plant, and lead guitarist, Jimmy Page, got together for two tours that came to Milwaukee in 1996 and 1998. I was fortunate enough to attend both of these fantastic shows.

See select ticket stubs from some of the shows I have attended at bangheader.com in the pictures link. Enter code bangheaderspics

Molly Hatchet and The Outlaws

On October 31, 1979, I attended the Molly Hatchet/ Outlaws Halloween concert at The Milwaukee Auditorium. (now The Miller High Life Theater) They had a costume contest and I dressed as a giant bong. It was fall, so I put some leaves in the bowl and blew smoke out of the top to give it a realistic effect. Very realistic- Some of the smoke was pot smoke!

Wheeling and Dealing Daze 1974-1987

I first sampled the sweet leaf (marijuana, that is) in the summer of '74, at the age of 15. My friend had a joint that we smoked in an alley near 35th and Wells St. I really enjoyed it and began smoking whenever there was a chance. He had a good source, so upon returning to high school for my sophomore year, I began dealing to make a little extra money, and promote access to something I strongly believe in.

 In all of my time in the business, I was never asked or required to join a gang, pay a "street tax", or pay protection money to stay in business. I had no turf to protect. My friends and customers were, for the most part, one and the same. As I say, "A friend with weed is a friend indeed." I was a completely independent business man.

There were a lot of stoners in school so sales were easy. At lunch, we would hang out across the street from school at a place called "The Lunch Box" to stay warm, play foosball, the juke box, and get a snack. Sometimes, the "Greasers" would pull up across the street with their hot rods. Someone would run out and pour some bleach on the road and they would do a big smoky burner.

There was a rooming house next to The Lunch Box that we called "The Palace", where we smoked pot in the hallway during the winter months. I conducted my business in the alley behind The Lunch Box. A guy we called "Burnout Taylor", asked to see a bag. When I gave it to him, he took off running and never came back.

Once, my partner in crime and I bought a bag that was very weak. It was not good enough to sell, so we rolled up two large cigar size joints, lit them up, walked down the street, and went into a convenience store. We were promptly asked to leave! Another time, I was with a few classmates on a class field trip to Madison. There, we lit up a joint in the UWM Student Union. A lady came up to us and said, "We have noticed a strange odor in this area of the building and we are going to have to ask you to leave."

Unfortunately, one of my best friends decided to take 12 hits of acid at once and was never the same. He showed up at my parent's house while we were having dinner, wanting to listen to music. I took him upstairs to my bedroom, turned on the music, and gave him headphones. Shortly after I returned to the table, our whole family could hear him singing loudly to the music and banging his foot on the floor.

My First Big Bust

Apparently, all of my new, long haired friends had gotten my parents suspicious, so they searched my room. They found 10 ounces of marijuana. My dad asked his detective friend at the coffee shop what to do. He said, "The best thing to do is turn him in." When I came home from school the next day, four police officers came marching up to my room. They took my pot and me to the Police Station. I spent a day and a half in juvenile lockup and got a short period of "informal" probation. After that, I didn't talk to my father for almost a year. I also cut his picture out of all the pictures I could find of us together and threw them away. I never quit selling pot. I just hid it better. Back then it only cost $140.00 a pound and I could sell it for $15.00 an ounce, $10.00 for a lid (two thirds of an ounce), or $5.00 for a nickel (one third of an ounce).

One time, my friend's connections didn't have a scale and sold us what he had as a quarter pound for $40.00. When we broke it up, there was a large rock in the middle but after that was removed there was still three quarters of a pound of pot. We made a killing on that deal!

Start The Day Off With White Cross

The next year I transferred to a high school that was much closer to home. Sometimes, to get my day going, I would crush up some White Cross pills (Speed) and snort them right off of my desk in 1st hour English class. At lunch, I would walk out the front door, cross the street, pull out a bag, hold it up and yell, "Does anybody want to buy some pot?" This school also had a large group of "Freaks." We would all congregate in a circle in the field across from school to smoke at lunch. In the winter, we would crowd into the bathroom of the Purple Martin gas station (now a McDonald's), or my house paint, dark green, 1963 Dodge Dart car with a push button transmission, and red vinyl interior, to smoke. I had the second lunch hour. Sometimes, in the winter, I would let my friends who had the first lunch hour sit in my car to smoke pot. I heard one time they had 10 people in there. I had a "Cold Toke" bong as standard equipment in my glove box. At lunch, we would fill it up with snow and drive around a ritzy area nearby and get high.

Once the hood came flying open while I was driving the Dart on the Highland Ave. bridge near Miller Brewery in the middle of winter. I did a 360, but was able to maintain control. Many a great time was had in that car. It finally met its demise on the way to Brian Shank's New Year's Eve party. It slid on some ice on a sharp corner and hit a light pole head on just half a block from Brian's house. I left the car and went to the party anyway!

We also had some beer parties at a nearby park. Once the police caught us and took us back to school. I dumped an ounce of pot under their car seat to avoid getting caught. Due to being stoned and sometimes drunk after lunch, afternoon classes were frequently cut. The next day, the office would send a pass to my class telling me to go to the office. I would just leave the building and skip out again instead of facing hard questions in the office. When I lost my books, I had to go to the lost and found which was in the assistant principals office. When I arrived he asked, "What's your name son?" When I told him, he raised his voice and said, "Oh Mr. Bangheader! I've been meaning to talk to you for quite some time now, sit down!" Fortunately, the bell rang and he went out in the hallway to keep an eye on the other students. I snuck out when he was looking the other way and he never caught up with me again.

Even though I was making some extra cash, I still continued working a large newspaper route and a part time job at a gas station after school. A couple of dealers would stop in at the gas station regularly. They had all kinds of pills and Angel Dust for sale. If I smelled pot coming from one of my newspaper customer's apartments, I would ask them if they wanted to buy some.

Stoned Sunday 6-8-75

The managers of one of the buildings on my newspaper route were hippies and we became fast friends. They let me use their kitchen to bake some marijuana brownies for The Rolling Stones concert at the Milwaukee County Stadium on June 8, 1975. We did our paper routes that Sunday morning, and went to the Stadium early to get in line for good grass seats. We arrived at 6am. The gates did not open until 10am. All of my friends, except one, smoked marijuana. He was kind of a mooch. You will hear more about him later in, "Christopher the Cheapskate". We told him we forgot to put marijuana in the brownies and when we turned our backs he ate 5 or 6. A short time later he left to go to the bathroom and did not come back. We found him about 100 feet away staring into space. When we brought him back to our group, he laid down and passed out for 3 hours. No harm no foul. He woke up just as the gates were being opened. This was the first huge show I saw with 54,000 people in attendance. Rufus, and The Eagles were the opening bands. Joe Walsh had just joined The Eagles and he popped up and played Rocky Mountain Way.

Several weeks later, we had a surreal experience during the Pink Floyd concert at the same venue. It was raining lightly during the show. While they were singing the verse, "I'll see you on the dark side of the moon", the rain stopped, the clouds cleared, and a full moon appeared over the stadium. The crowd went crazy cheering with joy. Ironically, the band never knew until after the show why everyone started cheering so loudly during that song since they were covered and their backs were facing the moon. A flaming plane came flying down on a wire from the top of the stadium and crashed on the stage during the show. The sound system was incredible, with speaker towers in all four corners creating complete surround sound. When they played "Money",you could hear the sound going from one tower to the next in perfect synchronization.

This was the first time I took LSD. It became my favorite drug to take at concerts, because it enhances the senses, causing the music, lighting, and visual effects to seem so much better, and you can drink beer all night without getting drunk. Beer just takes the edge off of the acid's effects. During my dealing daze, I encountered many different kinds of LSD, or Acid, as it is more commonly known. There were little pills that some called barrels. These included orange ones called Orange Sunshine, and purple ones called Purple Microdot. There was paper called blotter. Once I got several sheets of blotter which had 100 hits per sheet. It had a little picture on each hit. The sheets I got were called Dancing Bear, because each sheet had a picture of a dancing bear, or maybe it was because it made you feel like a dancing bear! It was very good. Sometimes it came on different colored plastic-like sheets. That was called Window Pane.

Once I had a friend over when my parents weren't home. We were "hot knifing" hash in the kitchen. This entails heating up the ends of two butter knives, putting a small piece of hash between them and inhaling the smoke. He passed out after taking a hit and I had to catch him before he hit the floor. My mother always wondered why the ends of those knives were discolored!

Yearbook Quotes- Sophomore Year

1. To the school junkie. Be cool Bangheader.
2. To a burnout who can't keep his eyes open.
3. To Jerry, one of my many burnout buddies. Have a happy and high junior year.
4. Jerry- Good luck in the future, you'll need it!
5. Jerry- A fellow burnout- have fun and stay high- ZAP
6. Jerry, a burnout who can't wake up.
7. Jerry, you smoke, you drink, you're a burnout, you're a flunky, you're a big time freak. You got everything you ever wanted!
8. To Jerry, my Columbian dealer. Stay cool, and don't get too high this summer!
9. To a freaky looking person in my 7th hour class. Have a high summer.
10. To a guy that needs toothpicks to keep his eyes open.
11. To my fellow junkie, make a lot of money this summer!
12. To Jerry- The next time I see you on a bus when I am on a bus with my gang, I will rob you.
13. To a dealer who fronts pretty good weed, stay high this summer- Burnout Taylor
14. To Jerry- Hope you keep getting Columbian this summer, but don't get too burnt out.
15. To Jerry- a really funny person in Geometry. Good Luck, you're gonna need it.
16. To the most wonderful, handsome and intelligent person I ever met. John W. (US lying champion 71, 72, 73, 74, 75)
17. To Jerry, from a fellow burnout. Stay high all summer and have a joint on me.
18. Jerry- To Mr. know it all about dope. Have a high summer.
19. Jerry will always be a burnout.
20. To a kid I knew this year - take care and don't get too high.

Yearbook Quotes- Junior Year

1. To a burnout who is in my homeroom- Have a good summer. Do not get high.
2. Jerry- First hour was pretty decent. That time you put that Trower album on instead of the record for a filmstrip was alright. Take it easy over the summer and maybe I'll catch you at a concert.
3. To Jerry, it's been a high year but I'll still be around this summer.
4. Hows it going Jerry- Have fun this summer. Hope you find plenty of you know what.
5. I really don't know you too good, but you're pretty cool. Stay cool and don't get busted.
6. Jerry- To the world's greatest burnout-Have a great summer.
7. Jerry- To a great guy who always seems to be high. Take care and I'll see you at some concerts.
8. To Jerry who had a high time in Chicago- Farmer
9. Have fun this summer, get high a lot.
10. Jerry you're a real nice guy. I'm glad I got to know you at parties etc. I hope you have a nice high summer.
11. Jerry (NORML) I'm really glad I got to know ya this year. You're really sweet and I hope you never change. Maybe we can do some really heavy partying. Take care of yourself. Note: NORML was written in large letters on a shirt I frequently wore to school. It stands for National Organization For The Reform Of Marijuana Laws.
12. Jerry- You're a real Buzz. Have fun over the summer.
13. Jerry- You wouldn't believe how wasted I am. Party Hardy!
14. Jerry- It's been nice knowing you. Even though I haven't known you for a long time, you are a really crazy person.
15. Have a great summer and don't get too burned out or high.
16. Mr. Space High- Hows your summer going to be? I already

know. I bet you're glad we're out. It was fun having you in 7th hour. Thanks a lot man for sharing your Bugles (The Underground newspaper). They really helped pass the time. Hope to see you this summer, maybe at the site.

17. Jerry- Take it easy this summer. Don't get busted for anything that I would do.

When The Cat's Away...

I turned 18 just a few months after the start of my senior year and rented my own upper flat. That was a real party palace. Being a lover of live music, I attended many rock concerts. Unfortunately, unbeknownst to me, I had befriended a bad person. He was a new kid at school named Brian. He lived at St. Charles, which was a home for troubled teens. It seemed like he was a nice enough guy, but there was a seamy underside to his character. Soon after establishing himself at school, he began stealing my pot customers. Then the upper flat I lived in started getting burglarized almost every time I went to a concert. One night, one of my real friends stopped over and found Brian climbing up my back porch. He knew when I would be gone because, believing he was a good friend whom I could trust, I told him that I was going to the concerts. He would then steal my pot and sell it to my customers. I also sold Brian a motorcycle. He never registered it and got a bunch of tickets. The police finally confiscated it and, since it was still in my name, they sent me a notice to appear in court if I wanted to get it back. I did. Explaining the situation, they greatly reduced the fines and released it back to me. A few weeks later, it was parked on the street and Brian stole it. Fortunately, my friend knew where he lived and we went over and stole it back.

Around this time I ate some Peyote Buttons, putting them in a mint milkshake to disguise the horrible taste. A half hour later, I threw up and started hallucinating. I thought a green waterfall was coming out of my mouth!

One night, I was riding around drinking, smoking pot, and snorting coke in my friend's car. When we arrived at another friend's house, I couldn't get the door lock open so I bent over and yanked on it with my teeth. It broke one right off! Now I have a bridge there!

I was also working part time delivering rental furniture during my senior year. One day, we finished early and decided to go on a tour at the nearby Pabst brewery. They gave us three free beers at the end and I took a couple of Valium pills. Now, too messed up to go directly back to the store, I hopped on the freeway with the truck and promptly sideswiped someone. The police did not even smell the alcohol on my breath, nor did they notice I was messed up. They just wrote up the accident and let me go. The only time I ever shot a drug into my veins was during this time. A guy I worked with invited me over to "hit" some coke. He injected me. All I felt was dizzy and sick. That was enough shooting up for me.

After finishing my senior year of high school, I continued to sell pot and work. I no longer sold pot in the open. Since I was friends with many smokers, there was a ready supply of customers. They called me, and I would deliver to their residence, or they would come to mine. I ran my business like a call girl, not a streetwalker.

Jerry's Drug Store

A friend introduced me to "John", who delivered pizza. When I called him, he would bring me a pizza and a pound. I was selling whatever I could get my hands on…pot, coke, acid, speed, downers, and hash were all on the menu.

Once, after scoring a pound of pot, I was bringing it home in a lightweight backpack which I had attached to the luggage rack on my motorcycle. Somehow, it came loose and slipped onto one of my mufflers. When I got home, all that was left was a little pot and some plastic melted together on my muffler!

One night I heard a crash and found that someone I knew had "accidentally" broken the glass on my front door, leaving me with no security. I invited him in and we took some Valium he brought and drank some beer. With that combination, you feel like your body has become a liquid. I woke up in the morning with a gun to my head and someone demanding to know where the drugs and money were. I said I didn't have any. They found twenty 100 dollar bills under a checker board on the floor next to my bed, but missed four pounds of pot that was hidden in the oven. I had never been robbed at gunpoint and it was really scary. Not scary enough to make me quit though. I even called the police. The police found several tri-beam scales that Brian had stolen from our high school and stashed at my place. They just confiscated the scales. I am sure that their presence helped them figure out why I got robbed. Later on, I figured out that my "friend" who had broken the glass set me up to be robbed. He also introduced me to a female Wisconsin Department of Justice drug enforcement agent without my knowledge. She would set me up for my second big bust. I was just too friendly with everyone and it bit me in the ass. My "friend", who brought all of this trouble to me, was someone my friends and I picked up hitchhiking and befriended.

Even after a good friend from high school was robbed and killed while selling some coke at age 20, I didn't stop. The money was just too good. As I got more customers and needed a bigger supply, "John" introduced me to his boss and supplier. When the boss injured his back, he asked me if I would like to move into his swanky apartment to help out with his dogs. I looked up to big dealers so I said, "Hell yeah." He would just make a call and someone would show up with a 40-50 pound bale and we would spend the afternoon breaking it up into pounds.

He had a friend who was into opiates, and I bought some brown heroin from him. I snorted it, and about 5 minutes later, my head started involuntarily jerking forward and backward. That lasted about half an hour. After that, I got the runs and sat on the throne for an hour. Not a fun experience, and the last time I ever used that drug.

Cocaine Catastrophe
Unfortunately, my new roommate had a bad cocaine habit. Every night when we were hanging out, he would offer me some for free. After a couple of weeks he said, "Do you want to split a gram?" I replied, "Sure." After that, I was paying for it. Less than a month after that, we each started buying our own gram every night. That part of my life is kind of hazy. After doing all that coke, we would stay up half the night and then sleep away the day to recover. I had become addicted. He had very good connections for coke. Unfortunately, the undercover female Wisconsin Department of Justice officer I had

unknowingly been introduced to set me up. She was able to get me to sell her 3 ounces of coke. As we were making the deal, she and her "boyfriend" pulled out guns and we were arrested.

We didn't even know what we had. The coke tested out at 86% pure, which meant we could have cut it several times and kept a bunch for ourselves if we had known what we were doing. That was the biggest deal I had ever done and I was busted... ten days in the county jail and then probation. The girl who supplied the coke was in our apartment during the bust and was arrested too. She ended up committing suicide before her court date. My roommate got a tongue lashing from the judge, who was his uncle, and ended up with probation. His uncle went on to get a reputation as the judge who groped women in the elevator of the courthouse.

At 19, I had snorted my lifetime supply of cocaine. After getting busted, I never used or sold it again. For a time, I quit dealing completely and started working full time. These jobs included a furniture warehouse, a submarine sandwich shop, and selling furniture. My probation officer told me that my drug testing was only for coke so I could still enjoy smoking pot without a worry. I guess I wasn't cut out for real jobs because I couldn't seem to get up on time to keep any job for more than a year. By the time I was 21, I was selling pot again. I stopped dealing the other drugs but became more involved in selling marijuana and it's more potent derivative, hashish when it was available.

Happy New Year !

On December 31, 1981, I attended a friend's New Year's Eve party. She said there would be a lot of people who wanted to buy pot, so I brought a quarter pound. That evening I took some LSD and decided to balance the veggie platter on my head. It fell to the floor. I proceeded to get down on my hands and knees and eat the vegetables off the floor. Later I went for a walk outside in the snow in my bare feet.

I owned and operated a snow removal business at this time and, due to a large snowfall that evening, I had to go directly from the party to work. After, picking up a friend to help, and my snowblower, we headed toward our first job. The police saw the snowblower in the trunk and apparently thought it was stolen, so they pulled us over. My friend was sober, so as soon as we stopped I said, "switch" and we switched seats. The cops pulled us out of the car and searched us. Unfortunately, no one at the party had bought any of the pot and they found it all. They kept insisting that they saw me driving but we both denied it. I was tossed in jail for the pot and for refusing to tell them who I was.

When they left me alone in the interrogation room, I took a couple of Valium pills that they hadn't found and passed out. They finally found out who I was from my fingerprints and charged me with possession and obstruction of justice. Fortunately, the male DA was sweet on my female public defender. He was trying to get her to go out with him. At my first court appearance, he got up and stated, "The stop was questionable and the search was definitely improper" and all of the charges were dropped.

Fry House Follies

Two friends and I rented a house on Fratney St. that we called the Fratney Fry House. We got a German Shepard from the shelter and named him Fire. Since it was a four bedroom place and there were just three of us, he got his own bedroom. There were no worries about being robbed or burglarized with him around. He thought he was so strong that he would go up to parked cars with metal bumpers and start biting them.

I threw a huge party there in the spring of 1982, shortly before leaving on my 11 week motorcycle trip. We had five half barrels. People would throw brats through Fire's window and he ate every one.... probably about 15. As evening approached, I took my best friends up to my bedroom and passed out the Dancing Bear LSD. Things got really wild then. I stood on the kitchen table and lit 3 joints at one time (See picture opposite page) among other crazy antics.

We ended up burning quite a bit of our next door neighbor's firewood in a large planter in the back yard. The next day I gave them several cases of beer for repayment. The police came several times because of noise complaints, and we always turned the music down until they were gone.

Even our landlord started buying pot from me.

Jerry- Tripping, Drunk, and about to be very Stoned

Fire- Waiting for another Brat!

I was a social beast and attended parties whenever possible. That summer I attended a party in Jackson, WI. Arriving on my motorcycle, I drank and smoked all day long. When it was time to go home, I could barely walk. Staggering onto my bike, I kept telling myself, "concentrate on the road, you're really drunk" for the entire 28 mile ride. Somehow, amazingly, I made it home in one piece.

When I returned from my 11 week motorcycle trip out west in 1982, I rented an apartment on the east side. The landlord was not quite finished remodeling the unit when I moved in so I met "Jeff", the painter. We both liked to smoke pot and I told Jeff that I needed a connection. He introduced me to Scott. Scott was able to deliver whatever I needed, and soon I was buying 10 pounds at a time.

One time I was leaving his house with 10 pounds in a speaker box strapped to the back of my motorcycle. I got pulled over on North Avenue in Wauwatosa for speeding. The officer was looking very suspiciously at the box when I realized that I knew him. He had dated a former boss of mine and attended the company Christmas party. He let me off with a verbal warning and did not check the box. Wow, that was a relief and a very close call!

The problem with Scott was he liked to make some extra money by putting an ounce of seeds in every pound which made it harder to sell. One day, when I was at his apartment, he introduced me to his friend, Mike. When Scott stepped out of the room, Mike handed me a piece of paper with his phone number and said, "call me." After that, I didn't have to deal with Scott or his seedy pot. Mike was able to get me as much as I wanted, at better prices, and it came straight from the bale.

With a great supply readily available, I was able to step up my business. My customers could buy anything from a quarter ounce to ten pounds. I developed the reputation of being a "Pot Snob" because I would only smoke and sell high quality marijuana, and I offered a 100% refund on the unused portion if anyone was dissatisfied with the quality. No one ever was. Everyone always got exactly the amount they paid for too, so I guess you could say I was an honest dealer.

One of my childhood friends went to The University of Wisconsin - Milwaukee that fall and moved into the dorms. He introduced me to his suite mates, they introduced me to their friends, and, before I knew it, I had many new customers. My new friends in the dorms affectionately nicknamed me Uncle Jerry.

During this period, I was active in community volunteering, working at a shelter for runaway teens, and organizing activities for seniors at a retirement home. No, I did not sell or give pot to the runaways. One day, I ordered a movie from the library called "Candid Candid Camera" to show at the retirement home. I thought it would be something funny. When I turned on the projector, the film started out with a man knocking on a door, the door opened, and there stood a naked lady. I was embarrassed and shut off the projector. The older ladies at the home surprised me when they said, "Turn it back on, we want to see it!"

One day, when I returned from volunteering, there was a knock on the door. When I opened it partially with the chain on, two black men who a customer had brought over the day before without my permission, forced their way in. I ran into the bedroom, grabbed my gun from under the mattress, and fired at them, but it didn't shoot. One of them pulled out a large shiny gun and pointed it at me. The other man pistol whipped me with a smaller gun. They kept demanding that I give them my drugs and money. I said, "I don't have anything" several times. Eventually, they found a large wad of cash in my pants pocket. I threw a large rock at them, out of my 2nd floor window, and just missed hitting one of them as they were escaping on the street. That was really scary!

Another memorable incident occurred in the same apartment when I heard a loud squealing noise in front of the building. I ran to the window and saw a car flying down Farwell Ave. upside down.

Not long after that, I moved to an upper flat a few blocks away. The living room was my waiting room, with up to ten people waiting at a time, and the spare bedroom was my office. I would usher people in individually and weigh out whatever they wanted on the spot. Some of my friends got paranoid on Friday evenings because of all the police cars parked just down the block. There was no need to worry. They were just getting a Fish Fry at Al Calderone Club on the corner where "Ma" would pinch everyone on the cheek. I even gave out free bags of pot for Christmas presents to my best customers.

I had some interesting customers including doctors, lawyers, an NFL football player, and one of Kato Kaelin's brothers, who would always ask me to throw in an extra bud for "The Gipper". Then there was Dennis. He was a trust fund kid who spent lavishly when his check came every three months. He was even known to rent a limo, be driven around downtown, and throw $100.00 bills out of the window just to watch people go after them. Two months later, he would be broke and need a "front" until his next check arrived.

Once, one of my customers asked me for directions. As I was giving them to her, she interrupted me and said, "It's not a freeway car." Another customer had an older car that could be started without a key. Someone in his neighborhood was driving it and parking it back in the same spot, thinking he wouldn't notice. The only problem was they did not put gas in it, so he put a sign on the dash board that said, "If you're going to use the car, please put some gas in."

Business was great, and at one point one of my friends said, "You're living like a king and looking like one too" because of the weight I had gained. I didn't even have to pay for drinks. I would just give my bartender a nice bud, and all my cocktails were on the house. It was around this time that I started drinking Blind Russians, which became my favorite drink.

Bale Boy

I was now getting my pot in 40 pound bales and selling thousands of dollars worth every week. Things were not going as well in my personal life. My girlfriend had a big drinking problem. We would be at a party and someone would tell me that she was lying on the floor in the other room. One morning, I went into the kitchen cabinet to get some cereal and

Jerry with 40 pound bale

found an open, cold can of beer she had quickly stashed when I came out of the shower. That was the straw that broke the camel's back. I moved out and went back to my old apartment.

Less than a year later, Mike said he was quitting the business. I had to hustle to find another supplier. Fortunately, one of my friends knew a guy who brought loads back from Belize, hidden in the roof of a school bus. We rented a Lincoln Town Car and went up to Minneapolis to meet him. He took us to his storage locker where he had over 100 pounds just lying on the floor. I only wanted 50, but he said that he was leaving for another trip to Belize and I should take it all and pay for the rest after it was sold.

A few weeks later, I got a call from my previous dealer, Mike. He said he had some friends coming in from out of town and they needed 50 pounds. I had never sold anywhere near that quantity at one time, but he had been my supplier for several years, until recently, so I trusted him completely. He showed up at 10 in the morning and said they wanted to see a sample.

The Big Bust

About half an hour after he left with the sample, there was a knock on my door. I looked through the peep hole and saw some men in suits that I didn't know, so I did not open the door. They said they were the GAS Company and broke down the door with guns drawn. It was the Wisconsin Department of Justice. Unbeknownst to me, Mike got busted and was setting up his friends and associates to get his charges dropped. They forced me to the floor and handcuffed me. While I was handcuffed on the floor, Mike showed up, acting like nothing had happened, and they handcuffed him too. I was immediately 90% sure that it was Mike who had set me up. I never did deals before noon. His leaving with the "sample" a half hour before the cops showed up, and his being handcuffed just because he "showed up" at my place, were both very telling.

I was taken downtown, where I was offered a deal. Turn in 3 people who were the same level I was, or one really big dealer

95

and I wouldn't be charged. I agreed to work with them so they would let me go that day. I named several people in my phone book as big dealers, even though, in reality, they were just personal use customers. They released me but I had to call and "check in" with them everyday.

Mike started following me around after my release. That really made me suspicious. I believe he thought I was so stupid that he could set me up yet again. I avoided him and even drove to a police station once to get him off my back. He turned out to be a muscle bound dirt bag jock, who didn't even smoke pot. He was just in it for the money.

After this, I was 99% sure he had set me up, so I said I would cooperate, and gave the Department of Justice his name and told them he was the biggest dealer I knew. Their response was, "We already have him." Hearing that removed any minuscule doubt that he was the snitch.

Getting busted really sucked. For the first time in my life, I had just scored a full pound of Afghani Black Hash with the Nepal seal stamped on it, and the cops got that too. I tried to contact the lawyer who represented me when I was busted with coke when I was 19. Back then, he was a long haired public defender who told me about smoking pot in the courthouse after hours. He loved the piece I had written during my 10 days in jail titled "City Lights County Bars", and we kidded around a lot. Seven years later, he was a judge in a nearby county. When he didn't return my phone calls, I showed up in his courtroom hoping he could refer me to a good lawyer. In the seven years since I last saw him, he had completely changed mentally and physically. Now he was dumpy, balding, and less than hospitable. I believe he did not want to acknowledge that he ever knew me. I waited until the courtroom had cleared and approached the bench. He said, "Jerry, you can't just walk in here like this. I'm a judge now." He did not give me a referral. In the next election, he lost his judgeship!

Didn't Snitch

I never gave the Department of Justice any useful information and, a few months later, they charged me. I pled guilty and threw myself on the mercy of the court. The judge ordered a pre-sentence report. The examiner reported that I was "sophisticated", and my behavior was "manipulative."

At sentencing, the judge said,"A lot of people come in front of me and say they were not the big guy- well Mr. Bangheader, you were." She sentenced me to two and a half years in prison. At that time, everyone sentenced to state prison in Wisconsin automatically got one third of their sentence off for good behavior, so the maximum amount of time I was required to serve was 20 months. Six months later, my lawyer got my sentence reduced by 6 months so the maximum I would have to serve was 16 months.

You really find out who your friends are after that. I thought Bob was one of my best friends. He agreed to help my girlfriend move my belongings to my parent's house. He needed to borrow my car the day before, so he could get to my apartment. My girlfriend let him, and he promptly absconded with it. He never showed up to help move. My Dad, and a real friend, finally tracked him down a week later, still driving my car, and got it back. He couldn't be charged with stealing it, since she gave it to him.

97

To The Can Man

I had just turned 27 and was headed to prison. My first stop
was The Milwaukee County Jail, awaiting transfer to the State
Prison System. There I was, put in a cell with a 19 year old
black guy, who was in for murder. He told me, "You're going
to get fucked by someone." My response was, "Yeah, not by
you." After that, he didn't bother me.

Then I was transferred to a cell block with 5 cells and about 20
people. One of the guys was in for a parole violation. He had
been released from prison and was at a halfway house when he
took off to go smoke some crack. Thank God I had never
gotten into that. It seems to have a very powerful and negative
effect on people's behavior.

After 5 days, it was off to Dodge Correctional Institute, a
maximum security prison in Waupun, WI. I spent 35 days there
in a small cell with two other inmates. For a time, one of my
cell mates was a crazy man. He was talking about his friend.
He said, "I stole his soul and left him a note" and "I loaned
Jesus my personality". One of the other guys in the cell was so
freaked out by him that he complained to the guards and they
removed him. Other cell mates I had there included a black guy
from Racine who shot a guy because he was "messing" with
his girlfriend, and a totally naive white guy from small town
Minnesota who ran a red light in his semi and killed someone.
He said one time a girl tried to give him a BJ and he told her
"Get away from there", and he wiped his penis off with toilet
paper after he urinated.

The next stop was the Minimum Security Bunkhouse, also in
Waupun. This minimum security prison is more like a military

barracks than a prison. There were no cells or bars and just a 6 foot chain link fence surrounding the yard with no guard towers or barbed wire. We could use the yard to walk, run, or exercise anytime we had free time during the day. If you had money in your account,which I did, you could order a variety of things from candy bars to chips to every kind of soda and tobacco product. Visitors could bring you treats, too. After each visiting day, there was a lot of pot smoking going on in the TV room, which was enclosed with glass. The beds were separated by 4 foot high partitions, and you could have your own TV and Walkman music player. The minute I walked in the door, the guards asked me if I had a driver's license and if I knew how to drive stick. It was yes to both questions. Then they pointed at an old covered Army truck and said, "Starting tomorrow, you will be driving that truck around town."

I was assigned to the State Garage, and began driving the truck into the big maximum security prison, also known as "The Wall", to pick up food from their bakery and bring it back to the Bunkhouse. When I went in, the guards would open one huge set of gates. After pulling in, they closed them behind me. They then checked me and the truck for any contraband. A couple of the guards were real imposing hard-asses. They always threatened to strip search me but never did. Then the second set of gates was opened and I would drive up to the dock. When I wasn't driving, I would sit around the garage and read magazines.

Since I was handling food and delivering it to our kitchen, I was always able to get extra treats. The worst thing about prison is the other criminals you are in contact with on a daily basis. Many are violent, hardened, lifetime lawbreakers. At

The Bunkhouse, many had done lots of hard time at maximum security prisons and had now been moved to minimum security, since they were getting close to their mandatory release date. As close as they were to release, some hopped over the fence and escaped shortly after arriving. They had been locked up for so long that they couldn't wait another few months for freedom, even if it meant going back to maximum security and more time when they got caught.

After long incarcerations, many inmates developed very bad attitudes. I was attacked by several inmates because their perception was that I had disrespected them. I was standing in the cafeteria talking to a guy I knew who was sitting at a table. Another inmate said, "Stop breathing on my food." I replied, "I'm not breathing on your food." He caught me in the hallway after dinner and punched me in the mouth. Incidents like that happened to me several times. Fortunately, I was never seriously injured or sexually assaulted.

Some of the inmates asked me what I was in for. I didn't want to admit that it was drug dealing, because I was afraid they might look me up after we got out and try to rob me. So I proclaimed loudly, "I'm a pimp. I've got three hoes in the back seat and a punk in the trunk." That was a respected profession to them. After that, some of them would frequently say, "Ol' Bangheader the pimp," when they saw me.

My sentence was relatively short, so I applied for a transfer to a work camp where I could work at a business and keep most of the money I earned. Just two months after arriving at The Bunkhouse, I was transferred to Thompson work camp, just east of Madison, and got a job at a Mexican restaurant.

Thompson did not have any fences, and we could go for walks, or run across the street on an oval and have bonfires in back. I worked a lot and time passed fairly quickly.

I then applied for a transfer to a work release center in Milwaukee. I got it, and ended up serving half my sentence at St. John's, which is now The Women's Center near St. John's Cathedral in downtown Milwaukee. There I had my own room and room key. I could crank up my boom box and watch my own TV. I got a third shift job loading trucks at a produce company, and was allowed to take city buses to work 6 days a week.

Since I wasn't on a regular schedule, I was allowed to go to the cafeteria and eat anytime. Upon returning from work in the morning, I would frequently go to the cafeteria and eat a whole box of Cocoa Pebbles! On Saturday nights, we were not allowed to work. My buddy and I would hang out in his room, order pizza delivery from a local pizzeria, and watch Saturday Night Live.

After about a week, I realized that no one was following me to the bus stop, so I got my car and parked it a few blocks away. Driving my car to work gave me an extra hour before and after work to go over to my girlfriend's place and have some fun, or go to a restaurant and get a good meal. About once a week, I would hang out with a friend at his place, having a couple beers and smoking a little pot before work.

One day one of the guards locked his keys in his car. I was able to get his car open with a clothes hanger. He was very grateful and the next Saturday night, when I was watching TV in my room, he knocked on the door, tossed me a joint and said, "Have a great night!"

When one of the drivers at work quit, they started having me drive a truck to the airport in the middle of the night to deliver produce to Sky Chefs. One night, before leaving for work, I was asked to give a urine sample. Back in those days it couldn't be tested immediately. It had to be sent out. I drank a lot of water before giving the sample to try to dilute any marijuana residue, but I wasn't sure that that would be good enough.

When I got out to go to work that evening, I drove directly to a friend's place who did not smoke pot and got some of his urine. On my drive to the airport that night, I stopped at St John's. My friend, the guard, was on duty by himself, as usual. We went into the locked room where they kept the urine samples in a small refrigerator, took out my sample, dumped it in the toilet, and replaced it with my friend's urine. I came back clean!

Time went quickly there. I worked a lot of hours, since there was nothing better to do. Sometimes, I would be asked to work a second shift during the day making produce deliveries. When I was released in April of 1987, I had $5000.00 saved from working in prison. I had to pay room and board while working, but the $5000.00 was after all of those bills were paid.

Epilogue

I never had any regrets. I was never a slave to anyone and had the time and money to enjoy life.

Although I hate snitches or confidential informants, as the cops call them, it is probably a good thing that I got caught when I did. Unchecked, my business, undoubtedly, would have continued to grow and I may even have been subject to being charged under the Federal Kingpin statute, which has much longer sentences.

The guy that turned me in kept dealing. Every time he got caught, he would turn other people in to get off. Finally, the judge got sick of his antics, threw out his "deal", and gave him almost five years in federal prison. I found out about his bust and sentencing when I saw the article in our local newspaper. He will be looking over his shoulder for the rest of his life wondering if someone is coming to get even with him.

I took responsibility for my crimes and never implicated anyone else. It is a very good feeling to know that you never have to look over your shoulder or worry about someone seeking revenge. As of March, 2015, it has been 30 years since I was last arrested and, other than a few speeding tickets, my life has been free of any conflicts with the law. Since I got out of the drug business, I have never had a gun or any other weapon pulled on me.

After being released, I investigated starting several businesses with the money I had made in prison, settling on a Dating Service. It opened in November of 1987, and was in continuous operation until March, 1999, when I sold it and semi-retired to concentrate on real estate investing.

Celebrating Complete Freedom

After my release from prison in April of 1987, I was ready to make up for lost time and dove right into life. My friend Ken and I planned our first backpacking trip. We hiked across the entire island of Isle Royale National Park. Driving the 540 miles to Grand Portage, MN, we stayed, where else,-The Grand Portage Lodge, which is now The Grand Portage Lodge & Casino. The next morning, we boarded a small ferry to Isle Royale. Lake Superior can be quite rough and I got seasick during the ride. On the island, I came close enough to a moose to look each other right in the eyes! The hilly and rugged topography was spectacular. We even got to see a rare full red (Blood) moon come up one night. Someone had written, "The stoner's with the boner's were here," on one of the cabin walls that we stayed in. We could relate!

Later that summer my friend, Jim, and I biked the entire "76" trail going completely around Milwaukee County in one day. As you may have guessed, that's 76 miles. The trail has since been renamed The Oak Leaf Trail and is now much longer. I also hiked the entire 74 mile Tuscobia State Trail in northwestern Wisconsin in three days with another friend. The last day was the longest. We hiked 40 miles that day finishing around 11pm. To this day, that is the furthest I have ever walked in one day.

That fall, I threw my 29th birthday party at my favorite bar. I recorded 6 hours of music for the party, and took my stereo and four speakers to the bar. Many friends came to help me celebrate. My drink of choice that night was Jose Cuervo 1800. My friends were buying me shots left and right. Everything was great until the end of the night. When the fresh air hit me, I was way too drunk to walk the three blocks home. I crawled to the cab stand across the street and proceeded to light up a joint in the cab. Back at home, I prayed to the porcelain gods for hours.

Modern Love Anyone?

Settling down that fall, I started a dating service and named it Modern Love. Those were the days before online dating. Members would come into my office to view pictures, profiles and videos, and choose potential dates. About 90% of the members were ordinary people. There was a reason the other 10% couldn't get a date.

On his video, I asked one man, "What's your idea of a perfect woman?" He replied, "Well, as long as she cooks and cleans good and can keep her yap shut, she's alright with me!" I asked another man, "Are you looking for the perfect woman?" He replied," Well, there's only one perfect person that ever walked the earth and they crucified him, so I guess I don't want anyone who is perfect."

One of my most memorable clients was a man who wasn't meeting enough ladies to keep him happy. He got drunk one night, and left me a number of threatening messages that I found quite hilarious. (Larry Lashes Out- Audio #1-5) Another man came in and told me how lonely he was, and that at 40, he was still a virgin, but decided he wasn't ready to join yet. He never returned.

Many strange folks came through the door, but the majority were very nice. In just over 11 years in business, there were 40 marriages, including the beautiful Polish lady I married.

Dating Service On A Roll

SINGLE?

Would you like to meet someone special? Modern Love was created to help people find compatible partners at an affordable price. Consider these advantages:

• Confidential • Video or Non-Video • Personal
• Guaranteed Lowest Price • No Blind Dates
• See Pictures, Profiles and Videos

ONE YEAR ONLY $149.00

MODERN ♥ LOVE

MEET THE PEOPLE YOU WANT TO MEET

Free Brochure - Call 277-9954
Prospect Mall 2200 N. Prospect - Upper Level

My second 15 minutes of fame came just 13 months after opening this business. Trying to stump a tenacious and very friendly specialty advertising guy, I asked if he could put my ad on toilet paper. To my surprise, he returned a week later and said he could. I was in a corner now, so I placed an order for the minimum of 100 rolls. When they arrived, I got permission to place them in the restrooms of the mall that my business was in, along with several bars in the area. An associated press writer saw it in one of the bars and called me for an interview.

106

The article she wrote was released over the wire on December 10, 1988, and was published in many newspapers all over the world. That spawned radio interviews with several famous DJ's, including Larry Lujack in Chicago, and a radio station in Australia. I was the first person to advertise on toilet paper. There had been toilet paper with money printed on it, and some other novelty patterns, but never any legitimate advertising.

The Big Blaze

From June of 1987, to May, 1991, I lived in an upper flat on Oakland and Thomas with a roommate. On April 24, 1988, while watching TV in my living room, which faced east, the windows rattled like never before around 11pm. A few minutes later, a fire truck came down Oakland and turned east on Thomas. Opening the blinds, I saw flames shooting high into the sky and thought St. Mary's Hospital was on fire.

My roommate and I walked the few blocks to see the fire. Just as we arrived, the entire front facade of Larson's paint store collapsed into the street, almost landing on a fire truck. The fire was so hot and intense that the house next door to Larson's caught on fire in less than 10 minutes. Within a half hour, the flames had spread to the next building which was the huge and historic Century Hall. It was built in 1890. Although the outside was brick, once the roof ignited, fire spread inside, and all the wood, used to finish the interior and make it look so good, was ablaze. All three building were burned beyond repair.

The initial explosion, which caused my windows to rattle, measured 5.2 on the Richter scale at nearby UWM. The explosion was intentionally created. The owner of Fox Bay

Realty, who had his office in the paint store building, killed his wife and children. He then went into the basement of Larson's, disconnected a main gas pipe, left, and killed himself at a third location. When enough pressure built up, the gas ignited, and KABOOM! All the paint blew up. All told, up to 30 pieces of equipment and 165 firefighters fought the blaze all night. There were eight apartments above Larson's Paint Store. Fortunately, no one died there, or in the other buildings that burned.

I had my own bad experience with that man when I was his tenant. When I was moving out on the last day of the month, he came in while I was gone and changed the locks. He then refused to give me my deposit, claiming I left the place dirty. I threatened to take him to court, and he finally gave me a little over half back. Later, I learned he had a rep for doing that to many of his tenants. Maybe, that's why someone threw a brick through his office window several times.

Boy Your Gonna Carry That Weight A Long Way
In July of 1988, Ken and I set out on another backpacking trip. This time we flew to Seattle, WA. From there, we took the longest cab ride of our lives…. 155 miles, ten of which were on a very rough dirt road, to the remote North Fork Campground in The Olympic National Park. I had never arrived late at night at a campground in the middle of nowhere by cab. In fact, I had never arrived at any campground by cab before. We were the only ones there that evening. Go figure!

The next day, we set out for Three Lakes Camp. The 6.9 mile hike ascended around 3500ft. This was, by far, the biggest climb I had done in my life. We had not really planned for it either. As Ken said, "When you lay a map on the table, it is flat." The 12 pack of beer in my backpack did not help. Upon arrival, we could only find two of the Three Lakes, but that was good enough. I decided that I would not be lugging all that beer around for the rest of the trip, so I drank eight cans. The rest of the trip was not as strenuous! All our efforts were rewarded by a gorgeous full moon. It seemed like it was almost close enough to touch.

We enjoyed many mountain and glacier views while completely traversing the park from south to north. One backpacker we met had only a sleeping bag and beer in his backpack. Some other backpackers gave us a ride to town afterwards, and the very first thing we all wanted was a shower! I believe it felt better than any other before or since.

In July of 1989, my final backpacking experience was in the Twenty Mile area of The Great Smokey Mountain National Park. My friend, Heather, and I did the complete loop. Some of the highlights included seeing a large buck and a number of does near one of our campsites, Gregory Bald, and an evening side hike to Shuckstack fire tower to see the sunset. On the way back, we saw a mother bear with three cubs crossing the trail about thirty feet in front of us. We also encountered a group of park rangers with shotguns. They told us they were searching for wild pigs that were destroying the natural habitat.

Reckless Rafting
In 1991, I organized a rafting trip with 9 of my friends. We went to "Shotgun Eddy's" on the famous Wolf River. This is a very scenic section of river through an Indian reservation. My friend's wife was a member of a well known organization for people who have a very high IQ. She got scared, and jumped

out of the raft in the middle of a big rapid. I think more common sense questions should be added to the IQ test! She just got scraped up a bit so, at least, luck was on her side.

On another rafting trip at Shotgun Eddy's the following year, we met a drunk guy in the middle of the river who had lost his "friends" and asked us if we could give him a ride! We did. After he got off near the end, we took a wrong turn and ended up going toward a dam. As we approached, the current got stronger and we could not get to the shore. We had to grab the fence and let the raft go over the dam and into the ravine. The water wasn't very deep so we could walk to shore, but what a scare that was!

Wedding Bell Blues

I got married for the first and only time in July of 1993. My fiancée worked full time. Since I owned my own business and had time to make calls at work, the wedding planning fell on my shoulders.

We had a beautiful wedding with 110 invited dinner guests and two bands, including a "banjo" band that played during cocktail hour, and a seven piece band after dinner all for about $2000.00 That's the good news.

Here are the fiascoes that the joyous event, and its planning, entailed. First, one of my groomsmen moved to California. He informed me that he would be glad to come back for the wedding if I paid for his round trip plane ticket. I said, "No Thanks."

Soon thereafter, we found out the priest we had been meeting with to plan the wedding had gotten one of the parishioners pregnant and had been removed from his position.

Next, the lady who was doing our flowers called three weeks before the wedding and said she would not be able to do them because of a family emergency.

A week before the wedding, I called the photographer we had contracted with and found out his phone line was disconnected. Soon thereafter, I found out the post office box he had given us as his business address was closed. After scrambling to find a replacement photographer, I received a call two days before the wedding from a photographer the original one had hired to take his place. He hadn't burned us at all. He just moved out of town without notifying us.

When I went to pick up my tuxedo, it had not been altered correctly and there was no time to make any changes. The pant legs were too long, making me look like a penguin.

On to the rehearsal dinner, where my best man screwed up the toast by saying my ex- girlfriend's name instead of my fiancées. Fortunately, she was talking with someone and didn't notice.

At the wedding, the plan was for my nephew, who was four and the ring bearer, to walk down the aisle with my fiancée's niece, who was two and a half and the flower girl. My fiancée and I had both agreed that she was too young to walk down the aisle by herself. As I stood at the front of the church, a very strange thing happened. I saw my nephew come down the aisle by himself. He did fine. My fiancée's niece came next. She made it less than a quarter of the way, turned around and ran out. My fiancée and her sister had changed our plans at the last minute without my knowledge.

At the altar, I noticed the center candle of the unity candle, which we were supposed to light together, was already lit, so we lit our unity candle the opposite way it was supposed to be done. Our new priest had just returned from a long stint as a missionary and was unfamiliar with the right way to light the unity candle. Maybe that's why the marriage didn't last forever!

After the wedding, we drove down Wisconsin Avenue, which is the main drag in our city, in the rumble seat of a model A a good friend furnished. When we arrived at the lake to take pictures, several of our attendants were missing. One couple left our procession to run an errand and the car behind them had followed them.

At the reception, I noticed one table only had two people sitting at it. That was my new mother-in-law and new brother-in-law. All the rest of my wife's Polish friends did not show up, even though they sent in cards saying they would. Not to worry, my new mother-in-law had invited some other Polish people, without our knowledge, and they sat there.

Because we were leaving on a three week honeymoon the next day, we opted to stay at our house instead of a hotel that night. My new brother-in-law, the one whose wife changed the plans so her two and half year old daughter would walk down the aisle by herself, had gotten a spare key for our house from my new mother in law. When we arrived home that joyous night, none of the lights in the house would come on. After finding my flashlight, I found most of the light bulbs in the house were missing. Our doorknobs were covered with Vaseline, the toilets had cellophane over the seats, and the bathtub and bed were filled with cereal. That was a lot of fun to clean up at 3am. We did not consummate our marriage that night!

Other than all of these things, it was the best day of my life! At least both of the bands and most of our guests showed up and the food was hot. What more could I ask for?

Rapid Recovery

In 1993, I was canoeing with two friends on The Chippewa River. I was in the back of the canoe, my friend was partially reclined in the middle, with a full brim hat on, and his wife was in the front. A group of young guys in two canoes pulled up next to us and said "Do you have any pot?" I said "How much do you need?" They replied,"a joint or two." I pointed at my friend lounging in the middle and said, "Sorry, he'll only sell it by the pound." They were so blown away that they canoed away with no response!

My wife and I also canoed the wild Peshtigo River that summer. We were not prepared for a big rapid right away and our canoe got stuck on a tree. It filled with water and bent in half! When I pried it off the tree and got the water out, it snapped back in place. I guess the extra money I paid for my high quality Royalex boat was worth it. I am still using it today and the only evidence of that accident are the stretch marks on both sides in the middle.

Elevation Delegation

Just six months after meeting the lady who would become my wife, we took a trip out west. There, we discovered we both

113

enjoyed climbing mountains and reaching their summits. Climbing the relatively easy Harney Peak in the Black Hills of South Dakota wet our beaks for bigger and badder mountains.

We ended up getting engaged a week later on top of Mt. Washburn in Yellowstone National Park. Just as we made it to the fire tower at the summit, it began to rain. I waited until the sun peaked out and popped the question. Just then, the tower keeper came out. We told him we had just gotten engaged. He left and returned with two wine glasses and some wine. We had a perfect toast!

Our new love for mountain climbing continued throughout our relationship, and we did some climbing every summer. All told, in 14 years, we summited 22 peaks and almost reached the top of another four. We reached the summit of six mountains that were over 14,000 ft., more commonly known as 14ers, and the highest point in six states. If it wasn't for Chicken Out Ridge near the summit of Mt. Borah in Idaho, it would have been seven. On one day, we made it to the top of three 14ers in Colorado and, if not for a rapid decline in the weather which included hail and sleet, we would have made it to the top of a fourth.

The first 14,000 ft. mountain I ever summited on foot was Mt Elbert, the highest point in Colorado. It is a booty buster. We ascended 4,700 ft. in just 4 and a half miles. Less than two miles from the summit, I collapsed from total exhaustion. Then, I ate two peanut butter and honey sandwiches, some cookies, and an apple, got re-energized, and made it to the summit.

Mt. Whitney took us two attempts on two separate trips years apart. It is the highest peak in the lower 48 states and, at 21.4 miles, the longest round trip hike of all the mountains we climbed. On the first attempt, we did not get a good night's sleep due to our motel room being right across the street from a gas station where semis were stopping all night to get coffee, leaving their rigs running. Just before reaching the trail crest, where you can see the mountain ranges on both sides, I started getting a bad headache. By the time we got there, altitude sickness had engulfed me. It felt like someone had a vise on my head and I was throwing up. The only way to get better was to go back down. The further down I went the better I felt. By the time we got back to the room, the pain had subsided. Exhaustion and hunger were the only things left. I ate a whole pizza and passed out. Didn't hear any trucks that night!

The second attempt eleven years later was a success. We rented a room away from the road this time! Starting at 6am, we climbed 6,137ft., reaching the summit at 2:30pm. We spent an hour there relaxing and celebrating. My cell phone worked and, of course, mom got a call. We got back to the parking lot at 9:30pm using a flashlight. The hike was long in miles and hours, but not as steep as many other mountains we've climbed, and the scenery was spectacular. There are two campgrounds on the trail. If you win the lottery, which is held each year for those sites and backpack in, you can stay right on the trail. I'll take the motel thank you!

Some other notable summits include: Half Dome in Yosemite National. We climbed 4800 ft. in eight and a half miles, but it was worth every step. There are two great waterfalls to view on the way up and back. When you get to the base of the dome, there is a pile of gloves to choose from. Then you ascend an almost vertical set of cables, anchored by metal rods, all the way to the top. Breathtaking!

We also climbed the mountains on both the southern and northern terminus of The Appalachian Trail. Mt. Springer, on the southern end, is much easier. Mt. Katadin, on the north, is another mountain that took two visits to conquer. The climb is 4,200 ft. in 4.3 miles. Anytime you are approaching 1000 ft. per mile, you can be sure it is no cake walk. In the hiking world, we say "You have to pay for the views" with your body, that is, but I have never been disappointed. The feeling of accomplishment and the views at the top are incredible, and once you reach the top, most of the battle is won. As I like to tell people, "It's all downhill from here."

Although not as tall as the mountains in the west, The Adirondacks, in upstate New York, offer some fantastic views. One of the best hikes I have done there was Mt. Marcy. At 14.8 miles round trip, and an elevation gain of 3600ft., it is a full days hike. The views are spectacular, especially at the top. When you get there you will be standing at the highest point in New York State. Some other memorable peaks I have climbed in this area include Mt. Dix and Algonquin Pk. These trails have some sections which are much steeper than the Mt. Marcy trail, so if you want a bigger challenge, they definitely qualify. On the Algonquin Peak trail, you ascend almost 3,000ft. In four miles. Mt. Dix has a section that is almost vertical. To me, it seemed like the steepest trail that could be climbed without technical gear. There are many other peaks to climb in this area with a great variety of trail difficulties and lengths.

None of these mountain summits can be reached with a motor vehicle. If that is more your style, I have also driven to several gorgeous mountain tops, most notable are Mt. Mitchell, just off The Blue Ridge Parkway and the highest point east of The Mississippi River, and Mt. Evans and Pikes Peak in Colorado, which are both over 14.000 ft.

Mountains I Have Climbed

Name	Ascent	R/T Miles	Summit Elevation	State
1. Harney Peak	1,100	7.4	7,242	SD
2. Mt. Washburn	1,400	6.4	10,243	WY
3. Mt. Marcy	3,600	14.8	5,341	NY
4. Mt. Albert	2,904	7	3,776	QC
5. Yosemite Pt.	3,040	8.4	6,936	CA
6. Lassen Peak	2,000	5	10,457	CA
7. Mt. Elbert	4,700	9	14,433	CO
8. Mt. Springer	2,000	8	3,760	GA
9. Mt. LeConte	2,800	13.2	6,593	TN
10. Lookout Mt.	1,527	5	6,727	ID
11. Lazy Mt.	3,120	7	3,720	AK
12. Mt. Healy	1,700	8	5,716	AK
13. Algonquin Pk.	2,936	8	5,115	NY
14. Mt. Sherman	2,100	5.3	14,036	CO
15. Mt. Camerer	2,470	12	4,928	NC
16. Mt. Borah	5,262	7	12,662	ID
17. Half Dome	4,800	17	8,842	CA
18. Mt. Whitney	6,137	21.4	14,498	CA
19. Mt. Dix	3,000	13.6	4,867	NY
20. Mt. Katadin	4,200	8.6	5,268	ME
21-23. Mt. Lincoln,	3,831	7	14,286	CO

Mt. Democrat, & Mt. Cameron-All three in one day.

Twin Trips Of A Lifetime

This part of my story is more informative than entertaining, although it does have its moments. If you are planning a trip to Florida, Canada, or Alaska, or would like to learn more about these places, the next 18 pages should be worth your time. If not, the events of July 6 on pages 122 and 123 and "Lost in Alaska" on pages 124-133, should not be missed. Other stories continue on page 136.

Just a few months after turning 40, I sold my dating service and set out for some serious adventures. Unlike many of my trips, I kept a daily log on these trips. The first leg was a six week trip to Florida from April 6, 1999 to May 18, 1999. We camped in many State Parks, going down the Atlantic side all the way to Key West and back up the gulf side. We hiked, biked, canoed, tubed, beached, swam, boat toured, and theme parked our way through the entire state.

One of our favorite places was Myakka River State Park. They have a great boardwalk for birdwatching. You can also rent a canoe and canoe with alligators; they won't bother you-really! The nature trail is very nice and on and off road bicycling is excellent. While camping there, we had several unique experiences. With a special permit, you can hike in their preserve where we saw over 50 alligators in one place at "The Hole." That was incredible!

One evening a man took the site next to ours. He set his Styrofoam cooler on his picnic table, put his tent up, crawled in and passed out. Soon thereafter we heard a crash and a loud squeal. Raccoons had pushed his cooler off the table. It landed on a small raccoon's leg and he squealed loudly. We tried our best to wake the man up but he was out, so we put what was salvageable in his car. The next day we saw the small raccoon limping around. On another visit there, we saw a raccoon carrying someone's skillet into the woods.

Possession and use of alcoholic beverages in Florida State Parks is prohibited. There are signs posted, in addition to the list of rules given out, but each morning the recycle bin is filled with empty beer cans!

While canoeing on the Suwannee River, we encountered a nudist who lived in a tree house. He was partially covered by a fence so we didn't get the full exposure!

Some other high points of the trip included all you can eat lobster tails, crab legs, and a great variety of other seafood at Boston Lobster Feast in Orlando, visits to Sea World, Disneyland, and Universal Studios, and canoeing and swimming at Wekiwa State Park, where a domestic duck followed us from the rental shack and jumped into our canoe. Then he started rubbing my wife's back with his beak. When we tipped and lost our binoculars, he started diving in the water as if he was trying to help us find them! He rode with us all the way to our pick up point. The owner met us there and said, "Did you see my duck?" He rode on my wife's lap in the van on the ride back.

We also visited Siesta Key Beach, Big Bend Boardwalk in Cypress Preserve, took a boat tour in the Shark Valley area of Everglades National Park, took a glass bottom boat tour at John Pennekamp Coral Reef State Park, saw The Florida Keys and Key West, took a boat tour to Pelican Island National

Wildlife Refuge to see the White Pelicans, drove, sunbathed, and frolicked on Daytona Beach, drove and biked the Ormond Scenic Loop, collected shells, and watched the dolphins at Nokomis Beach, toured The Kennedy Space Center, and visited historic St. Augustine.

On To Alaska - Diary Notes

Less than three weeks after returning from Florida, we set out on an 8 week trip to Alaska. Leaving Milwaukee on June 6, 1999, our first stop was Theodore Roosevelt National Park. We saw a large herd of buffalo and many wild horses there.

The next stop was Glacier National Park. It was cold and windy! Going To The Sun Road was still closed due to snow and we almost froze in our tent. The next day we arrived in Canada, staying at Kootenay National Park, which is the gateway to the Canadian Rockies. June 9-12 were spent camping at Lake Louise in Banff National Park and exploring the area. We saw elk, bear, and bighorn sheep on The Bow Valley Parkway, and hiked Johnston Canyon, Stewart Canyon, all around Lake Louise and Rockbound Lake, with snow up to our knees for the last mile and a half of the five mile hike.

On to Yoho National Park, where we hiked around beautiful Emerald Lake and to Wapta Falls. We also biked the Great Divide Trail. A side trip to Banff found us in the crowded hot spring pool. There was a large moose walking around the downtown area.
June 13- Hiked around Moraine Lake to Athabasca Falls and The Maligne Canyon.
June 14-Climbed the Columbia Ice field at Athabasca Glacier.
June 15-Rafted the Athabasca River.

June 16-Hiked Mt. Edith Cavell to the base of the glacier.

I cannot say enough about the beauty of these National Parks in the Canadian Rockies. They are simply spectacular and something anyone who enjoys nature's wonders should experience at least once in their life.

June 17-Drove to Maligne Lake.
June 18-Hiked around Medicine Lake and drove to Ft. St. John.
June 19- Drove to Lizard Hot Springs. While basking in the natural hot spring there, we saw a moose.
 June 20-Drove to Whitehorse and saw a native Indian summer solstice ceremony.
June 21-Arrived in Alaska, camping at Moon Lake.
June 22- Drove to Fairbanks and stayed in the "North Pole" for three nights. Biked to Chena River Recreation Area on a very nice bike trail around the lake and beach.
June 25- Arrived in Denali National Park.
June 26- Took a bus tour of the park to Wonder Lake. It was 11 hours long, but completely worthwhile. We saw several grizzly bears up close, and lots of fantastic scenery. Our guide was also very informative. No cars are allowed on this road unless you have a reservation at a campground along the way, which is very hard to come by.
June 27-Rafted the Nanana River in the park.
June 28- Hiked Mt. Healy overlook trail.
June 29- Hiked other trails near the park entrance and had a fabulous salmon bake dinner.
June 30- Drove to Anchorage. The views of Mt. McKinley had been obscured by clouds for our entire visit to the park so it

was a real treat when they cleared the day we left. We had a great view of the summit from Denali State Park.

June 31-Camped at Chugach State Park and biked south from the park on a trail. Finally! Some long awaited ethnic food! We had a great Thai dinner at Siam Thai that night. Gas was $1.16 a gallon.

July1-4- Arrived at Cooper Creek Campground near The Russian and Kenai rivers. The red salmon were running in the famous Russian river and people were lined up shoulder to shoulder along the banks for blocks fishing. We gave it a try but were not able to haul any in. Our line was not strong enough and kept breaking. Back at the campground, our neighbor from Utah did much better. He gave us a huge red salmon that we ate for three days. That red salmon was the best fish I have ever tasted. That week we hiked to Juneau Falls and Trout Lake Cabin on The Reservation trail and biked to Russian Lake and Russian Falls to watch the salmon spawn. We also crossed The Russian River on a hand operated ferry.

July 5-Drove to Homer via Kenai and Captain Cook Park where we hiked. This is a gorgeous drive. Stopped at Anchor Point, which is the most westerly point you can drive in the USA. Drove to the ferry terminal in Homer. Nice view of the Coastal mountain range.

July 6- Drove to Seward, hiked on Exit Glacier and camped at a city park. Not many campers, but four young people near us were drinking and getting louder and louder as the night progressed. I stayed awake since I was not sure what they would do next. About midnight, I heard two guys fighting. One of them said "John, you broke my f-ing nose!" Then I heard someone run off and 30 seconds later a girl started yelling at the top of her lungs "Carrie! Carrie! Carrie, come back." That was repeated for about ten minutes. Finally, the police showed up and took the rest of them away. I was really mad because of all the disruption they had caused us. The next day, I took the grease they left in their frying pan and threw it on their tent. Karma came back and bit them in the ass!

July 7- Took a boat tour of Kenai Fjords National Park seeing Holgate and Surprise Glaciers, a humpback whale, porpoise, sea lions, otters, and puffins. They also served us a great Silver Salmon dinner.

July 8- Drove back to Anchorage, stopping at Portage Glacier.

July 9- Biked several city trails with nice views of the bay. Saw a moose with her calf on the Coastal Trail which begins in Earthquake Park.

July 10- Drove to Palmer. Took a short bike ride on the trail near Matanuska County Park to Knik Circle View and visited reindeer farm.

July 11- Climbed Lazy Mountain. Great views of Knik Arm and Mat Su Valley.

July 13- Climbed black and blue ice on Matanuska Glacier and picked salmon berries.

July 14- Biked on trail by the river in Valdez to two nice overlooks of the Alaska pipelines southern terminus. Took a six hour cruise from Valdez, which is known as "The Switzerland of America" and cruised on Prince William Sound to Columbia Glacier. Saw large "haul out" of sea lions, an eagle's nest, playful sea otter, fishermen netting a huge catch of Pink Salmon and great views of waterfalls and Valdez.

July 15- Drove toward Tok with views of Wrangell St. Elias National Park. Drove to Chitina and back, staying near Chrstouchina River and biked on the trail by the river.

July 16- Drove to Delta Junction.

July 17- Drove to Tors State Park on Chena Hot Springs Road. Took a short hike on Tors meadow trail.

Lost In Alaska

The 18th of July was a warm, pleasant, and sunny day. My wife and I had agreed to go for a 15 mile loop hike in the Chena River State Forest on the Tors trail which was conveniently located just across the road from our campground. The trail follows the Chena River for 1/4 of a mile. From there, it splits... the left branch goes to the bluffs, while the right branch follows a boardwalk through meadows and wetlands.

It was about noon when we began heading for the Tors. The Granite Tors are large individual granite rocks jutting out of the tundra. On our way out we bumped into the volunteer campground hosts and mentioned that we were headed for the Tors.

As we climbed over one ridge and then another, the views kept getting better and better. We could see the rock cliffs near our campground, distant bluffs and a few of the Tors. The trail was well marked with mileposts every two miles. At milepost #6, we stopped for a hardy lunch. After the steep climb, my two ham, cheese, and green pepper sandwiches disappeared quickly. My wife had no problem consuming a can of sardines on whole wheat. Great energy food!

Now above the tree line, we climbed across the Munson Ridge. Here the trail was marked by rock cairns. As we reached the Plain of Monuments, the trail leveled out. Crossing the tundra can be tricky since there are many wet crevices to avoid. The tors were now towering in front of us, each group having their own characteristics. One tor reminded me of an old Indian warrior with several missing teeth. A nice cabin with a bench and warming stove greeted us at mile 7. We paused briefly to sign the guest book and celebrate the fact that our climbing was over for the day, or at least we believed it was.

When we reached the South Tor we followed the trail to the left. After descending for about 1/2 mile, the trail narrowed significantly and was somewhat overgrown. Having been on several trails in Alaska that were similar to this, we were not alarmed. There was another group of tors below which seemed like a good sign. After reaching that out-cropping the trail became even harder to follow. At this point, my wife started insisting that we turn around and go back.

Determined not to climb back up, and wanting to complete the loop, I insisted that we continue. After all, even if we were a little off the trail, we would surely cross it on the way down. After reaching the bottom of the first hill with no sign of the trail, I decided it was time to follow a south heading on my compass. Even if we were lost, that heading would bring us back to the main road, I surmised. To my disappointment, we began to climb again. Over one ridge, then two, then three. Each time, I felt we would surely see the road only to be greeted by another ridge and more wilderness.

By this time, it was getting quite late, and the realization that we may have a longer trek than I had originally anticipated was starting to sink in. The bushwhacking, initially driven by adrenaline, was quickly losing its appeal. As our good fortune would have it, the midnight sun gave us plenty of light. Darkness, which is one of my wife's biggest fears in the wild, was not a factor.

As we reached the third valley, it was nearing midnight and a faint trickling sound could be heard in the distance. Was it the river near our campground? As we drew closer, there was no sign of a road but running water for sure. This was a small river, we thought. With aching feet and tired bodies we decided to stay the night on the river bank. At least we had long term survival supply number one... fresh water!

The fresh running water tasted excellent and any fear of waterborne bacteria quickly disappeared. Firewood was plentiful, the sky was clear and, soon thereafter, with a lighter, facial tissue, and pine branches, we had a roaring blaze going. The fire, in combination with our Gore-Tex rain gear, kept us nice and warm. Dinner consisted of a few pretzels rationed from the lunch we had packed. Using my backpack as a pillow, I was soon relaxing fairly comfortably on the rocky beach. Unfortunately, I had no contact lens solution with me so I chose not to remove my hard lenses or close my eyes. Surely, by the next day we would reach the road and my eyes would be able to rest.

Night was marked by a cloudy gray look in the sky and cooler temperatures between 2 and 5am. Just after 5am the skies began to get a reddish hue and the temperature rose out of the 40s. At 6am we began moving. An adrenaline surge pushed the urge for breakfast aside and a few pretzels had to ease the urge for food. Wanting a guaranteed water source, and noticing that the river was flowing in somewhat the same direction we wanted to go, we decided to follow it downstream. Thick grass, brush and uneven ground made it rough going.

Less than 30 minutes after departing, I stepped into a soft spot in the high grass and went crashing 5 feet down into the cold muddy water. Up to my neck, I quickly grabbed a branch and pulled myself onto shore. Our only canteen flew from my fingers and into the water. I tried to retrieve it, but the shoreline was too muddy to get a grip. Grabbing a stick, I hooked the strap just before it floated away.

With all my clothes soaked and muddy, I stripped naked. Partially prepared for anything, I had a backpacking towel, a pair of gym shorts, a ski cap, and my Gore-Tex rain gear wrapped in plastic in my day pack. Discarding my underwear, I wrung out my socks, emptied the water from my boots, dried off with the towel, and donned the rain suit. Not long after my plunge, we were rewarded with a light snack. Wild salmon and blueberry bushes started appearing all around us, and we spent a good half hour harvesting their tasty fruits. Continuing slowly through the treacherous terrain, I noticed that the river now seemed to be flowing in a westerly direction. Hopes of quickly finding the road, which I had been so optimistic about, began to fade. The reality that we may be very lost was hitting home hard. A feeling of depression encompassed me. Suddenly, I felt that that this would be a long term fight for survival. Our only hopes of rescue arose from the fact that the campground hosts saw us leave, knew where we originally intended to go, and would surely summon help and a search party by the next day.

The terrain looked better on the other side of the river but we were unable to cross. Eventually, we spotted a fallen tree and used it for a bridge. Instead of being better it was worse! Now there was not only heavy brush but small bluffs to scale.

Realizing that the trail is not always better on the other side of the river, we again searched for a safe crossing and eventually found another tree-bridge. In addition to the thick brush, high grass, and prickly wild rose bushes, there were many smaller creeks flowing into the river. Finding a place to cross them was quite challenging, since their banks were surrounded by deep mud. Often, we took a "leap of faith" hoping the opposite bank was firm. The large Alaskan mosquitoes loved this area and, if not for the Cutter and Afterbite we had stowed in our day packs, much of our flesh may have been consumed.

A trail would parallel the river making the going a little easier and bringing our hopes up. Then, just as quickly as it had appeared, it would end and it was back to bushwhacking. From time to time more berries would appear giving us a little snack. Along the river there were many signs of wildlife. Moose and bear footprints, droppings, and large areas of brush that had been compacted where a moose or bear had recently slept were all common sightings.

Early that afternoon, we spotted our first sign of civilization. What appeared to be a large plastic erosion control device was anchored by rope to the riverbank. I felt sure that we couldn't be far from help now. Shortly thereafter, a trail appeared and a small candy wrapper lay by it's side. The trail paralleled the river for fifteen minutes and petered out. After another half hour of bushwhacking, the trail would reappear. This scenario repeated itself for several hours. Each time our hopes would be raised only to be dashed. Several more of the same type of candy wrappers would appear sporadically. By mid- afternoon our river flowed into an even bigger river. Was this the Chena River which we had been hoping to find? There was a red marker ribbon tied to a tree on our side of the new river and another on the opposite shore.... another glimmer of hope. Again, the river seemed to run more north and west than south. This worried me. Was this river running north? If so it would eventually join the Yukon River, and we would be heading for the Arctic Ocean and nowhere land.

My wife's feet were aching after nine plus hours of walking, so we decided to look for a good gravel bar on the river to spend the night. Luck would have it that there weren't any nearby. As the river turned south, we saw our first sign of a current human presence. A strobe light was flashing from a hillside about three miles straight ahead. My heart started beating faster, and the adrenaline surged. Was this signal part of a search for us? I set my sights and compass for the source of the light and charged forward briefly. Unfortunately, my wife's feet were raw and she could travel no further. We found a gravel bar to rest where I hoped she would get a second wind. That never happened, and soon we were gathering wood to keep away the evening's cool air.

The sun was still warm and we lay down on the smooth gravel for an afternoon nap. In the distance, we could see, what appeared to be, a network of dirt roads on the hillsides and I was sure that they must connect to a main road. We could also hear what sounded like the roar of a motor in the distance from time to time. Was this a generator or a semi in the distance?? A large dead tree provided ample wood for the evening's fire and with a large roaring blaze we felt nice and toasty. My biggest problem now was being able to see well. I needed to remove my contact lenses after more than thirty hours in my eyes. With no saline solution, I put water in the case and popped them out. Better water than nothing at all and saline solution is probably mostly water anyway, I reasoned.

Dinner was the last few pretzels and a few leaves. By now, I had pushed most thoughts of food to the back of my mind. Through the night, we took turns resting while the other person tended the fire. By two am, we had a roaring blaze going and were both resting by the fire. The overcast sky began to lighten up about four am and I awoke to a light rain falling. It continued until eight am. We began alternating between rest and drying our rain gear by the fire. By eight am it had warmed up a bit and we decided to move toward the place where we had seen the strobe light in the distance.

Off came our boots and across the cold river we went. Ankle deep mud greeted us on the opposite shore. Rinsing our feet, we booted up and headed through the brush. To our dismay, swamps covered the area in which we were heading. Forty five minutes were wasted trying to find a safe crossing. Finally, a narrow gap to cross, a small ridge to climb, and we were on the open tundra… very thick tundra! Imagine hopping across one foot by one foot squares of grass that are spongy when stepped on with one to two foot deep crevices on all sides. The elevated and thick grass under our feet bent away with each step. Sometimes, we would try to hopscotch between the spongy, grassy patches only to find ourselves frequently falling in the cracks. Other times, we would try to wind our way through the narrow crevices until it got too wet. This went on for several painstaking miles. Needless to say, our progress was at a snail's pace. Our hard work was again rewarded by huge ripe blueberry bushes along the way. The hungrier we got, the better those berries tasted.

Suddenly, there was a large flare in the air. Were they signaling for us? As we drew closer, out of the clouds came three F-15 Air Force planes flying in close formation. Then another flare, and more planes. This must be some type of military exercise, we surmised. As we moved closer to the hill, which was the source of the flares, we heard voices. We yelled, "Hello, anyone out there?" but there was no reply. Determined to reach the source, we continued toward the hill. As we gained elevation, the tundra grew thinner and the crevices disappeared. Small trees began to cover the landscape. Following a pretty good animal trail, we climbed up the forested hill. At last a dirt road - our salvation! We reasoned that the military used it to reach the top of the hill to set off the flares and, if we followed it downhill, we would reach the main road. In the distance, we could see what appeared to be a large military base.

There were tire tracks in the mud so we must have been headed for the main road. Another river crossing, what looked like a tree stand, and the road abruptly ended. We turned around and went back across the river and up the hill. Now two soldiers were marching toward us. On the bridge we met. They were Japanese, with full military fatigues and camouflage on their faces. Was this a NATO base? We said, "We are lost, which way is the main road?" They just shrugged their shoulders, apparently not understanding us. Pointing in the direction from which we had just come, they said, "Danger!" Then pointing in the direction we were now headed they said, "No danger." They then continued on their way toward the "danger" area.

Continuing up the hill, we heard voices again-more Japanese, eight of them. We staggered up to them and said "We are lost, can you help us?" At least one of these men could understand a little English. Candy bars and chips came flying from their backpacks for our hungry stomachs. A map was retrieved from one of their jeeps and, soon, we were learning that we had headed way too far south and arrived at a remote combat training area of Eielson Air Force Base, south of Fairbanks. Two of the men offered to take us on the long, forty two mile ride back to the main base. Through the bumpy, winding, dirt military road, they drove. About halfway through the trip, we were met by an M.P. in a Humvee. He signaled for the Japanese to stop, and transferred us to his vehicle. Passing us Coca-Colas, he told us that if we had been lost in this area the following week, we would have had a much longer hike since the exercises being conducted on that part of the base would have been over. He also told us that they had just dropped a 500lb test bomb earlier that day in the area where the road ended and we turned around. That is why the Japanese soldiers had pointed to this area and said, "Danger!"

Back at the base, the airmen were very hospitable. More snacks, showers, and medical exams- all on Uncle Sam! We learned that our major mistake had been going south. I had been mistaken in my belief that we had originally started hiking on the north side of the main road. We had been heading straight south, just as my compass had shown, but north was the direction we should have been going. The airmen gave us a topographical map so we could see exactly where we had been. Then, the base commander arranged for two of his men to drive us the forty five miles back to our campground.

To celebrate surviving the Alaskan wilderness, we went out for dinner. Wanting to order everything on the menu, I settled for the Nacho appetizer and the Blackened Salmon dinner. My eyes were definitely bigger than my stomach, which had apparently shrunk. I couldn't even finish the nachos and soon we were enjoying a nice long sleep.

Our campground hosts had noticed that we did not return the first night and became concerned. When we didn't return on the second night, they reported us missing, and posted a sign asking if anyone had seen us and to notify them if they had. The State Police were going to start searching for us the day after we ran into the soldiers. The Fairbanks newspaper picked up on the story and printed a short article.

My take aways from this experience are: If it seems like you are lost, you probably are, so turn around and go back. If that is not possible stay put. The closer you are to the spot you originally started, the easier it will be for a search party to find you. Always carry a lighter. Without a fire each night we would have been much colder and wetter. I believe a fire also scares away animals that otherwise might attack you. Also, bring full rain gear, a good map, a small flashlight, a compass, a first aid kit, a mirror, a water filter and a hearty lunch even on day hikes. Finally, if you must get lost in Alaska, do it in the middle of summer when the chances of freezing to death are greatly reduced and it never gets completely dark.

Out Of The Woods- Diary Notes Continued

July 21- Rest and Recovery day. Spent time in the various hot spring pools at Chena Hot Springs Resort.

July 22- Wildlife drive on Chena Hot Springs Road. Saw a bear with three cubs crossing the road and a moose eating in the middle of the river.

July 23- Drove south from Fairbanks to Delta Junction and stayed in a cabin just north on Wrangell-St Elias National Park. There was rain-no view of the mountains.

July 24- Drove to Canada's Yukon Territory and Kluane Provincial Park staying at a bed and breakfast on Lake Kluane which is the largest lake in the Yukon Territory.

July 25- Drove to Haines, Alaska. We explored the town and two nearby state parks.

July 26- Saw an eagle catch and eat a fish in a state park and boarded an Alaska Marine Highway ferry. Got off at Juneau and camped at Mendenhall Glacier.

July 27- Drove all the roads in the Juneau and Douglas area. Had dinner and shopped in downtown Juneau.

July 28- Hiked the loop trail at Mendenhall Glacier. Great views. Saw the waterfall.

July 29-Biked north of the ferry dock. Nice road with great views of the islands. Left on the ferry at 5:30 pm. Saw a pod of whales and a small shark.

July 30- Stopped at Petersburg. Walked downtown. Stopped at Wrangell and walked petroglyph beach. The ferry is a great way to see the inside passage at a much more affordable price than a cruise ship. We had our own cabin and there was a restaurant on board. The sound of the motor was a little loud but the views more than made up for that. It is nice to be able to bring your car on board. You can take this ferry to

Washington state but we opted to see a little more of Canada and got off at Prince Rupert.

July 31. Drove to Prince George. Very nice and unusual mountains in this area.

August 1- Returned to Lake Louise for four days.

August 2- Hiked to Mirror and Agnes Lakes, Beehive, Six Glaciers and two teahouses. 10-12 mile total round trip hike.

August 3- Drove to Glacier and Revelstoke National Parks. Drove almost to the top of Mt. Revelstoke hiking the last half mile through snow since that section of the road was closed because of the heavy snow. There were great views in all directions. Hiked Cedar and Tall Trees Boardwalks.

August 4- Drove to Takakkaw Falls in Yoho National Park. Hiked around falls. This is a huge and angry looking waterfall.

August 5- Left for Calgary. Delayed from 11am to 5 pm by a mudslide that closed both roads leading south. There was a huge traffic backup.

August 6- Entered the USA at Havre, Montana's one man boarder post.

August 7 to 8-Drove back to Milwaukee arriving at 4 pm on the 8th.

All the places we visited on our Florida and Alaska trips were worth seeing. I cannot recall one of them that disappointed us. If you are able, visit these places and see as much as you can.

Under The Hood

I have had a number of interesting and, at times, scary incidents in the hood. Milwaukee has quite a large inner city area. I have always been an avid bicyclist and, frequently, find myself riding through the inner city to get where I want to go. Mind you, I avoid riding through this area at night so all of the following tales happened during the day. Here are my experiences in chronological order.

When I was 17, I was biking west on Vliet St. A car ran the stop sign on 14th St. and almost hit me. I yelled, "Hey, you almost hit me." The car stopped abruptly. A black man jumped out of the back seat, ran up, and punched me in the mouth.

I have been bicycling a lot more in the last twelve years and all of the following incidents happened during that time period.

When I was 46, I was heading east on Garfield St., just west of Martin Luther King Drive. A clothes hanger flew up at my bike as if it might have been kicked up by a car's tire or my bike tire. The next second, a beat up minivan with three black teenagers inside passed me. I kept an eye on them. They went around the block and came back at me. This time they threw a fishing tackle box at me. I barely avoided getting hit. I realized then that they had thrown the clothes hanger too. I was sure that they were going to come back again. Not wanting to take any chances, I ditched out onto a busy street and into a safer neighborhood.

In the last five years, I had someone yell at me from half a block away, "Get your white ass out of this neighborhood", and a middle aged black man with a goatee and fancy hat pull up next to me in his Coupe De Ville, look at me and say, "Honky."

As I was biking west around 32nd and Galena, a man standing in front of a house looked at me and said, "Fuck You" out of the blue. On that same ride, another black guy thought it would be funny to drive in the bike lane right at me pulling away just before he hit me.

On a summer day at 5pm in 2010, while biking south on 32nd St. between Wells St. and Wisconsin Ave., a car came to a screeching halt half a block ahead of me. A young black man got out of the back seat, braced a gun on the roof of the car and fired 6-8 shots into an apartment building parking lot. Everyone on the street, including yours truly, ran behind the closest house for cover. As quickly as it started, it was over and the car squealed off. As we were coming out from behind the house, a middle aged black man stated, "That's too early for shootin'!"

In the summer of 2014, a car full of young black people were driving in the bike lane eastbound on the North Avenue bridge. I was bicycling on the sidewalk across the street and yelled at them, "Get out of the bike lane!" several times. They hunted me down and the driver got out acting like he was going to attack me. He said, "What you gonna do now? What you wanna say now?" Fortunately, there was a lot of traffic around and I was able to cross the street and get out of there.

In 2015, I was driving my car on a main street in the inner city. A black woman pulled up next to me at the stop light and shook her fist at me. I opened my window to see what the problem was. She said, "What's your problem-you better take your medication." When the light changed, she took off and cut in front of me. I have no idea what she was upset about.

On several occasions while I was bicycling, black teenagers came running out into the street at me as if they were going to attack me and/or steal my bike. I am not sure if they were just trying to scare me or were serious about it, but in each instance, I sped up and they never caught me.

I believe a number of people who see me bicycling in the inner city think that I am an undercover police officer and have heard several of them yell, "Po-lice" or "5-0" just before I rode by.

White Trash Antics

A few of the people who live in the hood may have given me some problems but they do not have a monopoly on it. As you will see in "Baptized By Fire", I have had many more problems with white trash. In addition to those stories, here are some other experiences I have had with white trash punks.

When I was nine, I saw a young man dump a stolen car in front of our house, grab a brick, and smash the windows out. Two years later, I was riding my new Raleigh Chopper a couple of blocks from home when a teenager grabbed me by the neck and said, "Give me your bike!" I said, "Why?" Something spooked him and he let go and ran away.

In the last ten years, I was egged by a carload of teens while bicycling in the suburbs, and a white punk on a bicycle threw a tomato at me hitting me in the head near the Milwaukee river on the bike trail.

Twice in the summer of 2015, a carload full of white punks tried to bait and beat me. I didn't fall for it.

The first time I was bicycling southbound on a busy street on the near south side. A carload of white punks honked their horn at me for no good reason. When they stopped at a stop light, the passenger in front gave me a hand signal trying to get me to pull up next to them. Instead, I stopped behind their car. Even after the light changed they waited, hoping I would pull up next to them. I didn't. There were other cars waiting to go so eventually they took off.

Just a week later, and only a mile and a half away, I was getting a tan bicycling with my shirt off. Again, a carload full of white teenage punks went by. The front passenger yelled "That's nasty put your shirt on." This was on a side street and no one else was around. They stopped a half block up and waited for me. I ditched out onto another street and avoided them. They tracked me down four blocks away and started yelling "Put your shirt on" again. By this time I had gotten onto a busy street, so they were afraid to do anything to me.

I am quite sure if I had talked back to either of these groups or given them the chance, they would have beat me down. Those are real men... three or four teens on one middle aged man. That's what I call WTA- White trash antics.

Other Fowl Attacks

In the spring of 2014, I was bicycling on a bike trail that goes through a marsh in eastern Waukesha county. A Canadian goose was standing in the middle of the trail and was not getting out of my way. I put my hands under my armpits, flapped them up and down like wings, and yelled, "Kakaw Kakaw." The goose flew into the air and rammed into my side leaving me with a small bruise.

The following spring, while biking in the same spot, I encountered the same scenario. I tried to be more subtle than the previous spring and just called out, "passing." This time the goose flew into the air and came flying directly at my head. I put my arm up to deflect it. It rammed my arm causing me to veer off of the trail and ride right into the swamp where I landed face down in the muck. The goose watched me drag my bicycle and myself out of the swamp from a nearby patch of water. I swore at him as I picked the swamp grass out of my teeth and wrung out my clothes. I guess you could say that I was given "The bird!"

Christopher The Cheapskate

I have known a few frugal people in my life. There is nothing wrong with living below your means. Christopher took this to a whole new level. We met when I got a job at the paper shack at the age of twelve. After our newspaper delivery days were over, we remained friends, since we had a number of things in common.

At age 22, we were up north camping and went to a small restaurant for breakfast. He had the waitress running. His bill was $4.00. He put out 15cents for his tip. I said, "Chris, you are going to have to leave a little more than that, at least another quarter." He then put out a quarter and took back his 15cents!

We always took each other out for a modestly priced dinner on our birthdays, usually Mexican. On my birthday one year, he offered to pick up a pizza which we could eat at his place. He said, "You can have any toppings you want." I asked for three. When I arrived, the pizza only had one topping. He explained, "They don't have that special anymore."

On another birthday, he wanted to "surprise" me. He took me to a new submarine sandwich shop that only served cold subs and had no dining area. Presumably, I was supposed to eat a cold sub in the car for my birthday dinner that year. I refused and, after a lengthy discussion, he relented and took me to a Mexican restaurant.

We also gave each other small gifts such as a CD for Christmas and birthdays. Around Christmas one year, a group we both liked released a new CD. I bought it and gave it to him. He also bought it, but he made a copy of it on his computer for around 10cents, leaving out several songs because they were "ballads." One of the songs he left out was one of my favorites. He then copied the covers artwork in black and white on a copy machine and gave me that copy keeping the original for himself.

Once, one of his girlfriend's friends threw a birthday party for his girlfriend. He gave her a $5.00 tee shirt he had gotten at a discount store in Florida. Another time, he threw a birthday party for her and gave me a list of duties that I was to carry out

141

at the party like make sure the cooler was full of ice, go to the store if anything ran out, and tend the grill. I did it all and he did not even send me a thank you note or give me a little gift for all that help. Nothing!

When he helped me by doing a few hours of work at my rental property, I took him to a concert, paid for his ticket, and bought him beer all night. When a friend of mine and I helped him move, he furnished the beer!

I like to go to concerts early to see if I can find people with extra tickets that can be purchased at a discounted price. One show that my wife, Chris, and I went to was out of town. I furnished the transportation and gas. He agreed to bring 18 bottles of Heineken beer. I went looking for tickets while he and my wife sat by the car in the parking lot drinking beer. When I returned 40 minutes later, I told them I had only been able to find one ticket for $20.00. He said, "I'll take it." I guess he thought I had just been out there working for him for nothing. Shortly after that, he confessed that he had not held up his end of the bargain with the beer and had already drunk most of the Heineken while I was out looking for tickets.

Another time,while I was looking for tickets, a radio personality gave me two for free. We were early for the show but he insisted that we both guzzle our six packs and rush in to see the opening act of this all day show. He never even offered to buy me a beer or anything else for getting him in for free.

We would take turns getting together at each other's houses and the host would furnish the beer. Once he bought a "special beer" for his "pal Jerry." Problem was I did not like that brand.

Of course, he never asked me. He just assumed that since it was one of his favorites it should be mine, too.

If anything is free, he swoops in. He has made a boob of himself at a number of weddings when the drinks were free. He even drank until he got sick at several of them. Once, when he was at his company Christmas party, he got so drunk on the free drinks that he crashed his vehicle into an overhead traffic light pole and brought it down at a major intersection on his way home. He then took off. Someone followed him and the police caught up with him at home.

If the drinks are not free, it is quite the opposite. I had my birthday party at a bar one year. He never drinks at bars... too costly. He was not drinking at the party and one of my other friends told me he bought him a beer because he felt "sorry" for him! Soon after he finished it, he left.

Even though he is cheap with others, when it comes to himself it is another story. He has never driven a used vehicle since shortly after graduating from college. Just a few years ago, he had two brand new vehicles in his garage just for his personal use. He also had a brand new house built for himself and paid cash for it!

After the house was built, there were still things to do like install the dryer vent, two shower heads, and fix some plumbing problems. Since he didn't know how to do these things, he asked me to do them for him a number of times when I came over to watch Monday Night Football. No compensation for this work was ever offered, and on several occasions, it took up a considerable amount of my time.

Landlord Stories- Baptized By Fire

All of the tenants in these stories were of the white race unless otherwise indicated.

My wild experiences in the rental business began in February of 1996 when my wife and I bought a four family apartment building in Waukesha,WI Almost immediately, there was a vacancy.

 I was a trusting new landlord, so when my new prospect said he forgot his checkbook but would mail me the check and wanted to start moving in right away, I just checked to be sure he was employed and gave him the keys. The check never came and soon thereafter I was at the courthouse filing my first eviction. The lady at the Sheriff's office said, "Oh that's where Richard is living. He is wanted for 14 counts of forgery."

I knew he wouldn't be returning anytime soon, so I sent a couple of friends over to move his belongings into the basement. Later that afternoon, I went over and knocked on the door like nothing had happened. Hosea, the Hispanic man across the hall, who called his black male roommate from Haiti his "Pet," came running out and said, "He moved out this morning." I said, "Great, I'll just change the lock then." He never returned for any of his belongings.

When Hosea moved, under threat of eviction for non-payment of rent, he took my refrigerator with him. He must have forgotten that he told me he was on probation. I called his probation agent, got his new address, made a surprise visit and got my refrigerator back!

Pay The Rent Not- That's Scott

My next tough customer was Scott, who worked for a furniture company. He never paid rent to me, directly, once. I had to go collect it from his grandma or employer. He got so far behind that I took him to eviction court. There, he swore he would pay every cent he owed me and he and I signed an agreement requiring his employer to pay me a certain amount of money from his paycheck every week. The first week, they paid me the amount of money we had agreed on. The second week, they told me, "Scott is no longer honoring that agreement." That's when I went straight to court and evicted him. I will never forget what he said as he was being evicted, "Jerry, I can't believe you're doing this to me." Fortunately, he brought his own boxes because, even though the eviction movers quoted me a low price, when the bill came it was huge. They tried to charge me $3.00 each for the empty boxes they brought and used instead of the ones already there. That didn't fly.

Flaming Four Family

Less than a year later, one of the kids in the building was playing with matches and started some furniture in the basement on fire. Half of the building was burned badly. The fire went through a heating vent, flashed through a first floor apartment, blew out the rear windows, jumped up the outside of the building to the second floor, blew out those windows and completely burned that unit. The poor guy living in that upper unit didn't even have time to flush the toilet and barely escaped with his life.

Fortunately, no one was seriously injured and, other than the roof and it's framework, there was minimal structural damage so the entire building did not have to be rebuilt. It actually worked out well. Since my insurance covered the rent during the rebuilding, I didn't have to deal with any tenants for six months!

With newer, more modern units, I was able to increase the monthly rents by $75.00 a unit. After the rebuild, a mostly Hispanic crowd moved into the neighborhood. Most were new arrivals from Mexico. They paid their rent on time, for the most part, but there were many other problems. I would pick up many empty beer bottles on the lawn, and the next day it looked like nothing was picked up. Want to fry an egg? Where do you put the empty shell? Just pop your back door open and toss it out along with all those chicken bones and used lime slices when your beer is finished.

Locker Living

In one of the apartments, if I went there during the day, there would be four or five Hispanic guys sleeping in the living room. If I came back in the evening, it would be the same scene with different people. During this time, one guy was frequently hanging out in the hallway drinking beer near that apartment. I assumed he was staying there. Someone had piled a bunch of car rims in the front of a storage locker so no one could see in. One day it was unlocked and I looked in. There was a bed roll on the floor, pictures of someone's family on a shelf, and a bucket to use as a bathroom. Just then, a guy showed up and said he was there to visit his friend. I said, "Stick around, he is being evicted and will need some help." I found out the guy hanging out in the hallway was living in that locker and apparently using the hallway as his living room.

Cock A Doodle Doo

Later that year, I went down to the basement and found a live rooster tied to a post. That had to be one of the most unusual things I have ever encountered. There was even some food set out on the floor for it.

Party Hardy!

At least two of the units occupied by my Hispanic tenants also liked to throw parties in the basement. Twice, they unplugged the sump pump to plug in their music, never plugged it back in, and caused a flood. They also removed the smoke detectors many times, left piles of empty beer bottles 3 feet high, kicked holes in the walls and doors, discharged fire extinguishers, removed screens from their apartment and the hallway windows, and removed the light fixture outside in front of the building. I threatened to kick them out, but since they were basically just working kids with a wild streak on the weekends, I just raised their rent $50.00 a month every time they really pissed me off.

When I sold this property seven years later, one of the apartments was still occupied by these people and they were paying $150.00 a month more than anyone else. That was an extra $1800.00 a year in my pocket. I was willing to put up with a little extra grief for that kind of reward. They even offered to pay for new carpeting after five years, if I would install it. No problem!

Some of the other tricks a number of my Hispanic tenants employed included putting up posters to cover large holes they knocked in the walls, letting their children draw on the walls with Crayons, not letting me know when a handle came off of a faucet and just keeping a pliers handy to turn it on and off, and pouring grease down the sink, causing a brand new three inch drain pipe to completely fill with grease buildup in less than two years. If someone called and they needed to write a phone number down, they didn't use scratch paper. Oh no, they wrote it on the wall.

No Hope For Hope

Then there was a black woman, named Hope, that I took out of desperation from a shelter in the middle of winter. She did have a job and I got an extra half months security deposit. She paid her rent on time the first month because a church wrote the check for it. After that, she was never home when I came to collect. I would usually have to meet her in downtown Milwaukee a week or so later, just before I was going to file for her eviction in court. Then she would show up 15-20 minutes late most times.

Once, I got a call from the police that there was some kind of emergency at her apartment, but they "couldn't tell me" what it was. Either I must drive the 30 miles to come and let them into her unit, or they would break the door down. I went and found out she had left her 12 year old and 2 year old alone in the apartment for over 24 hours. Her estranged boyfriend had gotten word of it and made a child welfare call to the police. When they found that the girls had adequate food and water and no other issues, they left them there alone. In Wisconsin, that is legal if one of the children is at least 12, but it does not mean it is the right way to treat them.

Twice, I had to take her to Eviction Court for non-payment of the rent. Both times she didn't show up and I thought it would be a slam dunk. Not so fast. After arriving in Waukesha for an early morning court appearance, my case was the last to be called both times. When I was called, the bailiff said, "Hope has opted to appear by phone." I said, "I didn't know that was an option." Since she was not there with the money I was granted a writ of eviction. The first time, she got a church to ante up for her again but, the second time, she had apparently used up all of the community's good will and had to move out or be evicted. She moved out, leaving all of her worthless furniture, a filthy apartment, and an ant infestation behind.

More Mindless Maneuvers

When 95% of my Hispanic tenants moved out, the only notice I received was seeing a pile of their furniture in front of the building when I arrived to collect the rent. They knew by the condition they left their apartments in that no security deposit would be refunded, so they did not bother giving me the required 60 day notice.

My four family building was located at the end of a cul-de-sac. There were eleven other four family buildings on that street. Together, with some other four family buildings on nearby streets, we formed an association. We had shared parking lots and all of us chipped in for their maintenance. During this period, I received several letters from home owners that lived on streets adjoining these parking lots complaining about beer bottles, and garbage being thrown in their yards, late night music, partying in the parking lots, drug use and dealing, cars parked improperly in front of their driveways, abandoned vehicles, vandalism, harassment, and graffiti.

Nov. 13, 2002

Dear Property Owner;

I feel that you should be made aware that the homeowners in the
        area have become very unhappy with the behavior of some of your
tenants, and I do emphasize that it is only some of them. Our summer was
often ruined by partying in the   rking lots, beer bottles and
cans thrown over the fences into the back yards of our homes, and music so
loud we had no peace even in our homes with the doors closed.

Hopefully, these behaviors will slow with the coming of winter. However, I
must tell you that we do not intend to spend another spring and summer
unable to enjoy our lawns, and afraid to be outside. We are tired of being
unable to let our children and grandchildren play in the park our tax dollars
payed for because it is full of bullies, broken beer bottles and used condoms.
Therefore, the people in our area have organized and are spending this
winter trying to find solutions to this problem, in conjunction with the
Mayor and the police department.

One of the things we have agreed upon, is that you, as landlords, have some
responsibility in screening the people you rent to, and in communicating to
them that if they intend to reside here, they must also attempt to be good
neighbors.

Therefore, from now on, when we are forced to call the police to restore
peace, we will also be phoning you at your home if the offenders are
identified as your tenants. These calls will be made to inform you of
annoying behavior on the part of your tenants, regardless of the time of day
or night.

If you cannot find a way to encourage more neighborly behavior by your
tenants, our next step is to begin a legal battle to get all rent subsidies in your
area discontinued. After many years of working to pay for our homes and to
be good taxpaying citizens, we feel we have a right to enjoy our
neighborhood, to have peace in our homes, and to be able to use our parks
and walk down our streets without fear.
Please do what you can to help us restore peace to our neighborhood.

150

I'm sending this letter to you to ask for help in cleaning up our neighborhood and then continuing this work with your tenants. We live at
Ave. in Waukesha. We have lived here for 10 years. Over the past several years we have noticed that there has been a **NEGATIVE** change in the type of people moving into our area. These people litter on our property. Party in the back of our house until 2:00 or 3:00 am, with their ethnic music so loud we hear through closed windows and the air running. We witness drug dealings and the use of drugs and alcohol regularly from our property. Our properties have been vandalized and broke into. They tease and torment the animals and the elderly in the area. These people seem to park their vehicles wherever they want, they have parked directly in front of our driveway, leaving us to drive on **OUR** lawn and the curb to get out. Not to mention they leave their abandoned non-functional cars wherever they want up and down our streets. During the winter months vehicles are left on our streets for days, making snow removal difficult, driving and backing out of our driveways dangerous. These people have no respect for the homeowners in this area and what we are working so hard for. We have found out that there are a number of people living in this area that have police records. Approximately 70 parolees live in the surrounding apartments. Would you want to have your children being raised around this? We continually call the police throughout the year with our complaints, but spring and summer are the worst. It is now time to have you involved, you are the apartment owner. Now that we have your names and addresses, we will be contacting you regularly, especially during the warm months to help us deal with your tenants.

We have children of our own. I do not allow them to play outside alone nor walk up the street alone. The people who live in the apartments badger them, try to sell them drugs, my children and their friends are being harassed regularly. I worry about my children being left home alone. If you had to live with this from your so- called neighbors I think you would be just as concerned and irritated. We bought our home as an investment to move on and better ourselves, as I'm sure you did when you purchased the apartments. Also, to provide a safe and comfortable home for our children. Thanks to you and the people you have chosen to rent to, we know longer feel that we have what **YOU** have! We are asking for the owners to step up and take responsibility for your tenants. We are asking that you monitor the tenants regularly, checking on the properties, homeowners that they affect. Also, that you monitor the number of people living in each apartment. Many times it seems as though too many people and children are occupying the apartments. We are asking that each apartment owner get involved with the home owners to help us restore our community.

We all are aware of the unfavorable neighborhoods in Milwaukee and other communities, but we do not want to live like that. We want a peaceful, safe and pleasant neighborhood. We want our neighborhood back and will fight to have these problems dealt with. A playground was put in over at ', the jesture was commendable, but the result of it is disgusting. From the time it was built, the area was taken over by the tenants in the apartments. I've gone over only a handful of times, because it is not safe for our children to play. There is broken glass from beer and other alcohol bottles on the ground, used condoms have been found, older teens approach the children for favors or trying to sell drugs, the graffiti that was written on the insides of the tubes was absolutely filthy. Now since we, as a group have roared the school district has cleaned things up. Would you want your children to play in this attractive setting? We are demanding to have the right to raise our families in the same setting and environment as you have.

Suggestions? We would be open to any feed back you can give us, but remember, we live here, we know what goes on here every day. Maybe to help with the parking issues, charge the tenants the fee of what a parking permit would cost. We see **so many** unoccupied parking spaces in the apartment lots, why is this? Is there a fee charged to have more than one spot? With so many empty spaces, wouldn't it be better to have a little bit of money coming in regularly than being greedy and having no money come in? We do hold the apartment owners responsible for the behavior and actions of their tenants, because trustworthy, law abiding, honest people should be living here. We do hope some of our concerns can be addressed and solved. We will be waiting to hear from all of the apartment owners and what ideas they would have to help straighten things out here. We should not be forced to move from our homes. Many of us have worked very hard to get to where we are.

As an owner, I would have loved to have good tenants, but if your units are empty, you don't make any money. In that area, waiting for a "great" or even good tenant was just a waste of time. I even had several tenants move back to Mexico and leave their vehicles behind in the parking lot. Sometimes, I would push them onto the street so the city would tow them away.

Shots Fired One Down!

All of my previous problems seemed minuscule when the shooting began. Like most people living in a big city, I hear about shootings in the news all the time but when it happened on my property and involved my tenants it became much too real.

I, unknowingly, rented a unit to two gang members. By this time, I was checking prospective tenants records on a web site. One guy had one misdemeanor charge for graffiti, the other guy was completely clean. Their Hispanic female roommate was also clean and was a teacher with the Head Start program.

A short time after they moved in, someone spray painted a gang insignia on the side of my building and in the middle of the street, but I didn't know who. Then in August, 2006, one of my tenants was shot in front of my property by a rival gang member. The police found a tattoo on his body identifying him as a member of a specific gang. The entire cul-de-sac was closed by the police for a number of hours with at least 15 police cars responding. A possible suspect came running out less than a half hour after the shooting and was "tasered". About that same time, someone started yelling their gang affiliation out of a window in my building from the unit where the suspected gang members lived.

Soon thereafter, there was a second shooting in October, 2006, involving the same rival gangs. It occurred in front of my building where 4-5 children were playing. This time, no one was hit and the police apprehended the perpetrators a short time later. They were three Hispanic males, ranging in age from the late teens to the early twenties. In addition to the gun which they had thrown out of the car but was recovered by the police, they had three baseball bats, two knives, and cocaine. The shooter already had one conviction for shooting at someone else a few years earlier.

Shortly after the second shooting, the other members of the Building Association had a meeting. I was not notified or invited. They stipulated that I must evict the problem tenants. If proof of eviction was not provided in 10 days, I would be penalized $200.00 a day. If it still was not provided in 40 days the penalty would increase to $600.00 a day.

I didn't waste any time evicting them. That was quite the icing on the cake to finish off almost eleven years of ownership. Less than two months after the last shooting, I sold the building. Every time I showed the building, I went there an hour ahead of time to pick up all the garbage in the entire neighborhood.

The man who bought my building was a religious fanatic, and every time we met, I got a sermon. He bounced his check for the appraisal and I had to give the real estate company the $500.00 of earnest money he had given me to cover it. In the end, he bought my building for $280,000.00 with a total of $500.00 out of pocket. That is what you call being overextended. The bank filed for foreclosure of his mortgage for non-payment less than a year later, and the foreclosure was finalized just 13 months after I sold the building to him.

Double Trouble

I bought my second property five years after the first, just five months after returning from Alaska. It is an eight family building that, as of this writing, I still own. For almost six years I had two buildings. Like my first property, there were many situations to deal with right away. The former owner didn't care about maintaining the property or who he rented to. I believe some of the tenants I inherited were way behind on their rent. The only reason he didn't evict them was to make the building look better on paper to prospective buyers and the bank with a "full house."

This building was closer to my home and had mostly white tenants. I have not had any shootings there but as you will see, some of these tenants are quite adept at causing many different problems. The very first time I went to pick up the rent, not one of the tenants was there to pay me. I guess they were practicing the rule,"Don't pay your rent on time or you'll make the rest of us look bad." I picked up one full garbage can of dog poop from the lawn, and a couple more piles in the basement that day.

Right off the bat, there were problems with a number of the tenants. When I finally got a hold of the only black tenant three days later, he didn't have the rent. I explained that I would have to give him and his very pregnant girlfriend a 5 day notice to move or pay. He started pounding his fist on the counter and said, "I'm getting angry. You better leave or something bad is going to happen." I left, put the five day notice on their door and they moved out.

Vince Was In A Big Pinch

In a unit upstairs, I never did meet the tenant. Vince had already moved out without taking most of his belongings with him. Turns out, his girlfriend was pregnant and at the same time he had gotten another woman pregnant. He moved up north, presumably to get away from the whole situation. I went to court and got an order of eviction. Fortunately, girlfriend #1 was good enough to come and remove all of his belongings.

A third tenant said he did not have the rent but would pay everything he owed next month. I told him, "I don't run my business that way. If you don't have the rent this month it is very unlikely that you will have twice that amount next month." He didn't pay, so I evicted him. Less than a year later, he filed for bankruptcy and discharged his debt to me. When I went in to fix up his apartment, I found that he had dyed his carpeting red.

Coreen Careens Out Of Control

The third eviction in that first year came when one of the residents moved out and asked if it would be OK if his sister, Coreen, moved in. I said sure since I would not have to do any advertising or fix the place up. She moved in with her black boyfriend. They had been living in the inner city and brought roaches with them. The bugs quickly spread to other units. I hired an exterminator and let everyone know when they would have to be out of their apartment, and for how long.

When the exterminator came, Coreen and her boyfriend were not at home but their dog was. I had to borrow a cage and put him in the hallway. The exterminator set off the bombs, and I put a note on their door instructing them not to enter the unit until a certain time. He came home, ignored the note and went in while the bombs were going off. He was supposedly then rushed to the hospital with an asthma attack. Later that evening, Coreen went crazy in the hallway claiming this was all my fault and she was going to sue me. (Coreen Careens Out Of Control- Audio #6-7) Shortly thereafter, I evicted them for nonpayment of rent. Her boyfriend showed up in eviction court, but said nothing when the judge asked him if he had a legal defense to eviction. Their "lawyer", who Coreen had alluded to on the voice mail messages she left me, was nowhere in sight!

The next year was not quite as eventful with only two evictions. The first was Jim. I gave him a chance, even though he did not meet my minimum income requirements. He gave me a letter stating,"I appreciate the slack you have cut me" and went on to claim I "screwed" him. (See letter next page) The money he claims I "screwed him out of" was the court fees he was required to pay me back, because he forced me to take him to court.

DEAR JERRY

I AM WRITING THIS LETTER DUE TO THE
CHAIN OF EVENTS THAT HAVE RECENTLY TRANSPIRED.
YOU HAVE STATED ON NUMEROUS OCCASIONS THAT
THIS IS BUSSINESS NOT PERSONAL. THIS HAS FORCED
ME TO CHANGE MY APPROACH, AND VIEW THIS FROM
A MORE BUSSINES AND PROFESSIONAL MANNER.
UNDER NO CIRCUMSTANCES DOES THIS MEAN I
DON'T APPRECIATION THE SLACK YOU HAVE CUT ME.

YOU HAVE MADE A STATEMENT THAT YOU
WILL NOT PAY ANY LABOR COST FOR THE
BETTERMENT OF AN APARTMENT. (THE TERM
BETTERMENT MEANS ABOVE AND BEYOND
MINIMAL CODE REQUIREMENTS) THIS LABOR
STATEMENT YOU HAVE MADE SETS A PRESIDENT
AND DEFINES THE RULES OF OUR AGREEMENT.
IF YOU WILL NOT PAY FOR LABOR. YOU WILL NOT
BE PAID FOR ANY.

WHEN I MOVED IN YOU ASKED FOR
1 1/2 MONTHS SECURITY DEPOSIT WITH A 1/2
MONTH DEPOSIT TO BE RETURNED AFTER 90 DAYS.
THIS ADDITIONAL 1/2 MONTH WAS FOR FINANCIAL
PROTECTION OF YOU SO THAT YOU WOULD NOT
BE SCREWD FINANCIALLY. BASED ON YOUR
ACTIONS WITH COURT FEES I AM THE ONE WHO
NEEDS TO BE PROTECTED FROM YOU. YOU TOOK
ADVANTAGE OF ME WHEN I WAS STRUGGLING
FINANCIALLY. YOU TRIED TO SCREW ME WHEN
I WAS DOWN.

Another Snot Named Scott

Scott also came with the building. I guess I am lucky with people named Scott, who make me get the rent from someone else, because just like the Scott from my other property, he never paid the rent directly to me. I had to go get it from his mother or grandmother. Then he moved his girlfriend in without my knowledge. She sponge painted the entire unit in green, red and blue. In addition to the walls, she got paint all over the woodwork, tub surround, light fixtures, towel racks, closet doors, bathroom ceiling, and carpeting. His family got tired of supporting him, quit paying, and I evicted Scott and his girlfriend. It took three heavy coats of paint, applied with a three quarter inch nap roller, to cover their walls.

A few months later, while visiting the property, I found extension cords running from the hallway outlet, which I pay for, into two units. The utility had shut them off for non-payment so they just stole mine. I unplugged them and cut both cords in half!

City Hall Circus

That same year, my manager called on my birthday and said the city garbage truck had done some major damage to the parking lot. When I came over to check it out, I found a large area of the path to the dumpster damaged, and there was a large crater in front of the dumpster. I called the sanitation department and they said that there was a signed agreement on file holding them harmless for any damage to my property. I did not remember signing anything like that so I asked them to send me a copy. It never arrived because it didn't exist. When I called back, they said they would drop off some information in my mailbox. It basically said sue us. I got a lawyer and did.

I was first summoned to appear almost a year later in front of a committee, mostly made up of aldermen. In so many words, they called me a liar and said if I wanted to pursue this further, filing a case in small claims court was necessary. How naive I was. I thought they would just send someone to my property to verify the damage and a city crew to fix it. Things were about to get very ugly. There is a reason they say, "You can't fight city hall." The city said I was required to file my claim within 120 days and it must include two estimates for the repairs. I was not able to get those estimates in that time period because all of the asphalt contractors were closed for the winter and were not giving estimates. I did inform them of the damages within that time period and my intent to make a claim. They also produced a copy of an agreement holding the city harmless of any damages, signed by the previous owner, and claimed this agreement was binding on "the building" even though I had no prior knowledge of its existence.

During the time my lawsuit was going on, the city sent me a letter stating that if I did not sign an agreement holding them harmless of any damages, they would be discontinuing my garbage pickup. It was then that I told them to remove their dumpster from my property and hired a private company. They also sent a city inspector who ordered me to make the repairs before the lawsuit was settled, and they dragged the court proceedings out for over a year and a half using various legal tactics to postpone and delay hearings. To me it seemed like a clear effort to wear me down and increase my legal costs so I would give up and go away. I didn't.

In the end, the judge ruled against me because I didn't have a witness who actually saw the damage as it was being done. The city also claimed my testimony was unreliable because I had been convicted of a felony in the past. Ironically, I have been summoned by the county for jury duty twice, and served as a juror at a criminal trial once, so apparently, I am deemed honest and reliable enough to judge someone else. I guess, at least in my case, our local government's gold standard is the double standard!

Jail House George

Then came George, a middle aged, single man, who seemed fine until he got arrested and put in jail for the weekend, leaving his large dogs locked in the kitchen area of his apartment alone. I tried to get in to check on them and discovered that he had illegally changed the locks. Fortunately, I was able to climb through a window. I went over there, and walked and fed his dogs for the entire weekend. The dogs seemed surprised when I took them to the park across the street. I do not believe they ever walked that far before. Most of my tenants' idea of walking their dogs consists of opening the door and letting them run loose in the yard to go to the bathroom.

When he moved out, he left one of his vehicles on my property with a for sale sign on it. I thought it belonged to another tenant and didn't find out it was his until two months later. He also left a huge grease stain in the middle of the living room carpet, and had painted his hallway and master bedroom green. I do not allow tenants to do any painting without my permission, and then, only if they agree to repaint in the original color before moving out and I am sure they are qualified to do the job right.

Daunting Dawn

Dawn was the first of three tenants I had that were on SSI Disability. None of them worked out, and all of them caused major problems. The Government may deem them fit to live unsupervised on their own, but my experiences paint a completely different picture. They all needed advanced supervision which I am not willing, equipped, or trained to provide. All three submitted lengthy "Move In" lists with various problems that didn't exist, or were things that could be expected of a building that was 30+ years old. One of the biggest problems with the SSI Disability people I have rented to is, they didn't have a life, so they try to get into all of the other residents lives. After that, someone looks at someone else's significant other the wrong way, borrows something and doesn't return it, breaks something belonging to someone else, or any number of other scenarios, and there is a fight... mostly verbal, occasionally physical.

This happened a number of times with Dawn and her live in boyfriend, Mike. They also called me any time of the day or night with non-emergency issues, mostly created by them, did unauthorized painting, brought unauthorized and prohibited pets into their apartment, left piles of dirty laundry in the basement for days, damaged things in their unit like electrical outlets and switches, that under normal use should never be damaged, moved a third person in without permission, left their door unlocked allowing their dog to run free in the hallways and outside, and let another resident, who I had evicted, store his belonging in their basement locker. They also expected me to repair their damages at no charge.

After their one year lease was up, I raised their rent significantly, placing them in the "high maintenance" category. I also added additional restrictions like not calling me late at night for non-emergencies, no additional pets, no painting, and required a complete inspection of their unit with them having to pay for all needed repairs. Thank goodness that was enough to get them to move out. I didn't throw them out because she was "Handicapped", and I didn't want to be accused of treating her unfairly. They gave me their written notice in the middle of the month (which is illegal) stating "You will only get a half month's rent, not a full month's rent. You will not get a penny more, that's final." By then, she was calling herself Domonique instead of Dawn. Can you say cuckoo, cuckoo!

Pauline seemed like a nice lady who had a steady job. Two of her adult children lived with her. Her daughter was 18, and her son was 19. Neither one could keep a job for more than a few weeks. They were both on the strange side and, when Mom was at work, they would fight loudly and constantly pick on each other. I know this because I heard it in the hallway every time I was there. Her son also broke into a basement storage locker. He ran out of the building and down the street when another resident caught him in the act.

When Mom lost her job, I took them to eviction court. They moved out leaving almost everything behind including all of their furniture and a dirty diaper under a bed. I'm not sure where that came from since there were no small children living with them. Their bathtub was so filthy that it was completely black, and I had to use a razor blade scraper to get all the soap scum off. I do not believe they cleaned it once in the two years that they were there.

Ken and Kim decorated their unit by stapling plastic flowers to the wood trim all around the dining room's built in cabinets. Always a story instead of the rent, they moved out to avoid eviction just four months after moving in.

Mike and Julie Were Very Unruly

Mike and Julie were the building managers I inherited when I bought the property. Less than eight months after becoming their landlord, they had a 4th of July party and oh what a party it was. Fireworks were discharged inside in the hallway, and they disconnected the smoke detectors. When it started raining, they pulled their burning charcoal grill into the hallway and smoked up the whole building. Now that's a party!

Even though she never called the police until throwing Mike out and getting a restraining order, it is told that other residents heard him beating her frequently. Their next door neighbor

164

claimed he heard Mike forcing her to have sex with their large dog! When she kicked Mike out, a Hispanic man named Hosea moved in almost immediately. One day at noon, I stopped over and found Hosea outside, drunk and accusing our next door neighbor of throwing garbage into our dumpster. One evening, I stopped by and found Hosea drunk again, arguing with other residents. I also caught them running their apartment from my hallway electricity after theirs was turned off for non-payment. Less than six months after moving in, it was reported that Hosea was beating Julie, too.

They did not do their management duties well or frequently. When they moved out, I found out they had removed the wood baseboard trim in the entire unit, painted the built- in living room cabinets black from floor to ceiling, removed all of the master bedroom's carpeting, and the door to the master bathroom, broken two windows, and, created numerous large holes in the walls and doors. They had also installed steel security bars on the inside of their front door frame which had to be removed, their carpetless floor was so damaged with dog urine that special heavy duty chemicals were needed to remove the smell, and they left a storage locker full of junk behind. One of the other residents ran into Julie a few years ago and she thinks I am still storing that junk for her! I just looked her up on the Internet. Two years ago, which would have been ten years after moving out of my building, a man had taken out a restraining order against her. Go figure!

Larry's Rotten Rug Rats
Larry was a longtime tenant who never gave me any major problems. His kids, who moved in and out of his place at different times, were a different story. The first problem was

with his older son's girlfriend. As I mentioned earlier, one of the other residents brought a roach infestation into the building and I hired an exterminator to treat every unit. As required by law, I gave the residents plenty of advance notice. His girlfriend would not leave the apartment when the extermination was to begin. The exterminator lit the bombs and, instead of leaving right away, she grabbed one of them and threw it into the common hallway.

Then his daughter, Jennifer, moved in. Her black boyfriend didn't move in but he was around frequently. He did auto work in the parking lot, leaving a large pool of oil, ran an extension cord outside from my public outlet, parked illegally in the lot and driveway frequently, and got into conflicts with my tenants which culminated in him discharging one of my fire extinguishers on Dawn and Mike's front door. As a condition of her being allowed to continue living in the building, I required her to ban him from visiting. She told me that she got a restraining order against him, but I still received numerous reports of him visiting, as well as witnessing it myself. Finally, he was caught at my property with a license plate on his car that had been stolen from one of my tenant's vehicles in the parking lot. It was then that I told Larry either she goes or both of you go. She finally did.

Soon after that, his younger son moved in with his girlfriend, Denise. They wanted to rent the vacant apartment next to Dad but neither one had a job. They assured me that they both had jobs lined up and agreed to pay an extra month's security deposit from their "savings." Later, I learned the money had actually come from a cash advance on her credit card! I allow a maximum of two pets; dogs and cats only, but made an exception and let them keep their cat and two dogs.

Less than two months later, all of the common areas in the building started smelling like the bird house at the zoo. While doing a plumbing repair in their unit, I discovered where the bad smell was coming from. They had gotten two ferrets. I had to wash my clothes when I got home to get the smell out. I ordered them to get rid of the ferrets immediately. In addition to this, their neighbors were complaining about their constant late night fighting, profane language, and their barking dogs. Denise got so mad at me for making them get rid of the ferrets that she told several of her co-workers and a supervisor that she was planning on intentionally falling in the parking lot and suing me. She did, getting a lawyer and suing me via my insurance company. Fortunately, her employer and co- workers were very honest. They sent me a letter telling me about her scheme, which I forwarded to my insurance company.

I never heard any more about it until a year later when my insurance premiums went up significantly, and I went shopping for a new insurer. When they asked if I had any claims, I said, "No" assuming that no monies were paid for a fraudulent claim. They came back and said I did have a claim. Apparently, in my case, they did pay a fraudulent claim. I am assuming that route was the best for their bottom line. They paid her medical bills and did not even inform me.

When they moved out one month later, just before being evicted for non- payment of rent, I had to remove all of the flooring, carpeting, kitchen cabinets, and baseboards to get the smell out with an expensive odor blocking paint and cleaners. I also had to paint all the common areas of the building with the same paint. Turns out the smell was not only from the ferrets. They had also been locking their dogs in the kitchen for long periods when they weren't home and it became their bathroom.

With Jason and Lisa My Headaches Increasa

Jason and Lisa seemed like a nice young working couple who I rented to in late 2002. Everything went fine for over two years. Then their next door neighbor, Colleen, started complaining about their loud music at all hours. I talked to them about it many times and they would either lie and deny it, or say they would keep it down. Soon thereafter, Colleen started complaining about her car being egged, and the tires being slashed, and she moved out. She had attached around a hundred stick on stars that glow at night to the master bedroom ceiling. Those were a lot of fun to remove!

Not long after that, Paula, her boyfriend Chuck, and her two teenage sons from a previous relationship, moved into an apartment on the same floor where Jason and Lisa lived, and trouble followed. They had represented themselves as "family people" and were around 40, which is much older than most of my tenants. Both had decent jobs. Then I started getting calls. This doesn't work, that doesn't work. Problem was that most of the time I couldn't find a problem. Finally, Paula told me, "Chuck makes stuff up."

When Paula and Chuck were not home I could hear her younger son, who was 16, abusing their dog. He also pulled his truck right up onto the front lawn and washed it one day. Then her older son started hanging out in Jason and Lisa's apartment. The story I heard was that when Jason was away, he ask Lisa if he could see her tits. When Jason came home, she told him and a fight broke out between them. Then Paula and Chuck's car was egged, one of their tires was stolen, and they moved out.

Some of the damage I found when they moved included holes in brand new woodwork above the bedroom window, large burn holes and bare spots in brand new carpeting, a badly damaged door frame, and a door mat duct taped to the carpeting between the master bedroom and hallway. They did not give me the required notice to move either.

When I had a chance meeting with Paula at a supermarket two weeks later, she got nasty, accused me of cheating them out of their security deposit, and threatened to sue me. Fifteen minutes later, I got a call from her ex- husband, who was not a party in this matter. He stated, "Paula and Chuck know where you live and they will not let this go." I then sent them a letter telling them I considered that a threat, and if anything happened the police would be visiting them first. Nothing did. Just a lot of hot air blowing in the wind.

I Regretta Renting To Loretta
When nineteen year old Loretta moved into the apartment next to Jason and Lisa, it wasn't long before trouble started again. Loretta and her boyfriend had a fight, and he completely broke the door jamb to get into her apartment. She then got a restraining order and began calling the police claiming he had violated it. In one day, she made three separate calls claiming this. All were found to be baseless by the police. That same month, she also claimed there was a burglary in her unit (but nothing was taken), then a battery and another restraining order

violation. Again, the police found all of her claims to be baseless.

Hallway Havoc
In the same six week period, there was a fight in the hallway at 4am, which originated in Jason and Lisa's unit. The police were called to their unit for the late night noise and witnessed many people coming in and out. Jason was seen parading back and forth in front of the building with a stick over his shoulder, as if he was guarding something, he went knocking on a number of his neighbors' doors at 4am claiming there were "strange people in the building", he ran out of his unit and took a picture of another resident that he had had no prior contact with, and the police were called several times because of noise complaints and disturbances.

On February 15, the police were once again called by Loretta regarding loud screaming and yelling from Jason and Lisa's unit.. once at 5:35am, again that evening at 9:25pm,and again the next day at 8:03pm. Upon responding to the third complaint in less than two days, the police issued them a citation. The very next day they were called again because of a loud fight in the hallway between Jason, Lisa, and Loretta, presumably because Jason and Lisa were mad about getting the citation.

Feuding Frenzy
Just nine days later, all hell broke loose. Five police officers and two sergeants were called to the building for a fight with weapons. Jason had brandished a baseball bat, and Loretta had a sword. Thank God the police arrived before anyone was seriously injured. A week later, I received a letter from the city

informing me that if there were any more police calls or trouble, my property was in danger of being declared a "Nuisance Property", and that I must submit a plan to them outlining how I was going to abate these problems within 10 days. I immediately gave Jason and Lisa an eviction notice, and informed Loretta that one more unfounded police report would result in her eviction.

When Jason and Lisa moved out, they didn't take much with them. Lisa stated, "I hate moving" as she was putting a few dirty dishes in a bag. They didn't have a lot of furniture but they did leave a full size water bed and lots of clothing behind, including about 40 pairs of ladies shoes. The kitchen was packed with full garbage bags, and the sink was full of dirty dishes. The entire apartment was almost knee deep in empty fast food bags, and I found a crack pipe so I guess we know what time it was. They had also taken to drawing pictures on the walls. It was not art! Less than two weeks after moving out, Lisa died. She was just 26 years old.

The police calls from Loretta stopped, but the problems did not. I spent many hours on the phone with her mother, while she tried explaining to me why Loretta had such a screwed up childhood, and how I should be giving her a break. I got calls to repair things at her apartment that she broke, her friends and relatives visited frequently (and in great numbers), parking illegally and swearing profusely in the hallway. She ran the air conditioner in the middle of winter, left her rent with another tenant without telling me, left the back door open, and smoked in the hallway. When she had a baby, she decided that she and her visitors should all smoke in the hallway and put an ash tray there. One day when I was at the building, her apartment door was wide open and I could hear her 13 year old female relative swearing loudly like a sailor. F this, F that, those F-in F-in Mf-ers... Wow, 13 years old!

I do not give tenants keys to the back door. Loretta's friends and relatives would frequently, illegally park in the driveway by the back door. She would leave the door unlatched so they could get in. One day, when it was very windy, it is my belief that she left that door open. The wind completely broke it off of the building. It was a big heavy metal door. You cannot just go buy a new door like that. It is a special order item. It was less than two years old and now damaged beyond repair. I forced it back in the doorway, duct taped it in place, and put signs on both sides that said, "Danger! Do Not Open."

Two days later, the door had been opened and I found it lying on the ground. Loretta's dad, who was one of the main offenders parking illegally in back, was walking around with a large bandage on his head! Obviously, he didn't take the sign seriously, and with no hinges, when he pulled the door knob, the whole door came down on top of him! What I would have paid to actually see that happen. Priceless! When her lease was up, I jacked up her rent significantly and she moved. Good riddance!

Connie Cuts Up
Connie was a 50 something year old lady with a good job. She moved in with her daughter and granddaughter. Then she moved in her adult son. A few months later, she moved in a second adult daughter, without informing me, which was a violation of her rental agreement. I found out later that this dikey looking daughter was a registered sex offender who had

been convicted of improperly touching a child. I got a call from her downstairs neighbor saying water was leaking through the ceiling. It was coming from her fish tank! While repairing a faucet, I noticed a piece of duct tape on the toilet tank covering a large crack. She never informed me that they had damaged it. If I hadn't found this, there would have been a huge flood when the water eroded the tape loose. Then her daughter had another baby and they decided that all three smokers in their unit should smoke out in the hallway. Not to worry if the other residents didn't want to inhale their second hand smoke.

When she moved out, the unit was left filthy and several things were damaged. No one had ever broken an oven control valve before, and the kitchen sink sprayer was broken off. I found out she was moving when another landlord called for a reference. Without proper notice of moving, I charged her for my advertising costs, as is outlined in my rental agreement. She filed a complaint with The State Department of Consumer Justice in which she made a number of false claims against me. She claimed that she was informed of unsafe conditions before she agreed to rent from me, and that there were "unhealthy conditions as well as unsafe conditions in and around the building." She was never specific about any of these "conditions" because they did not exist. Her main complaint was that I improperly charged her for advertising. In the end I prevailed. Unlike most of my tenants, I know the laws pertaining to the rental business and I obey them. If I didn't, I would get sued and be in legal trouble frequently. I have never been taken to court by a tenant and, if I ever am, I will prevail because they will have no legal ground to stand on. Like Connie, some talk a big game, but talk is cheap!

Nicked Up and Waist Deep In The Marsha

Nick and Marsha were a young couple who both had new jobs and a baby on the way. They had been staying with her parents and needed a place of their own. Everything was OK for four months, and then they started bouncing checks. I got a notice from my bank that one of my checks had been returned for nonpayment. I had never bounced a check. It was then that I found out their check, which I had deposited in my checking account, had bounced. It took three weeks for the bank to let me know. They assured me it was all a big mistake by their bank. Then it happened again, and yet a third time. After that, I only accepted cash. About this time, Marsha started going around knocking on other residents doors asking if they had an extra beer. Then I found out Nick was a recovering heroin addict who was on Methadone. Some of his antics included overfilling the dumpster and recycle bins with uncrushed boxes, disposing of empty soda cans near his vehicle in the parking lot, leaving items in the common area, and leaving dirty laundry in the laundry room overnight. When they moved in, Nick asked if he could paint the baby's room. I was hesitant and told him about my past experiences. He assured me that he was a "professional" painter, would do a perfect job, and repaint in the original color when they moved out.

When they moved out, to avoid being evicted for nonpayment of the rent, he did not repaint and there was paint all over the carpeting and woodwork in the "baby's" room. They also promised to clean, but left the sinks, toilets, stove, and refrigerator filthy with juice and syrup spilled all over inside the refrigerator. The drain pipes were missing completely under one sink, a toilet seat was broken off, and they left a large desk, bookcase, love seat, and mattress behind which I

174

had to remove, as well as a number of items in their storage locker. The carpeting in the living room and master bedroom had numerous cigarette burn holes and there were about 60 nail holes in the walls. The mini blinds, which were new when they moved in 14 months earlier, were filthy, and they had installed some kind of security bar in the master bathroom, damaging the woodwork. Over eight years after they moved out, the police came to their former apartment looking for Nick!

Devil's Angel

Angel, and his girlfriend, Christina, were a Hispanic couple. When they moved in, everything seemed fine for a while. Then I started receiving complaints about loud physical fighting, and the police were called several times. On one of these occasions, dingbat Nick, from the previous story, called the police but sent them to the wrong apartment so nothing was done. Soon thereafter, Christina moved out.

In short order, the police were called again because Angel's neighbors heard him torturing his dog. They heard the dog yelping and crying for long periods of time and being thrown against the wall. I told him he must either get rid of the dog, or I would be reporting him to Animal Control. He got rid of it. He also liked to leave his windows wide open all day in the middle of winter, and overloaded the dumpsters with large items causing the building to miss its' pickup.

When he moved in, there were 21 working light bulbs in his apartment. When he moved out, not one light bulb in the whole apartment worked and neither did one of the toilets. The toilet had to be completely removed and replaced. After breaking it apart, I found a child's toy lodged deep inside. The kitchen sink was clogged, a two piece queen box/mattress was left behind, the master bedroom door was damaged beyond repair, all of the appliances were filthy, some of the living room floor molding, which had just been replaced before they moved in, had been removed, and I discovered one of the reasons his dog had been crying. He had been locking it in the bathroom for long periods of time. The stench of urine was overwhelming, and the lower corners of the vanity doors were chewed off.

As you can see, many tenants do their own unique damage. Eric, Brianna, and their children were no exception. Once, when Eric didn't have the rent, he called the police claiming he had gone out to get something out of his car in the middle of the night, and someone came up behind him, put something to his head and robbed him. My building is not located in the type of neighborhood where things like that happen, and I do not believe someone was standing out in the cold, in the middle of the night, hoping someone would show up to rob.

When they moved out, the living room carpeting was covered with gum and candy and the walls were covered with Crayon, pencil, magic marker, and nail polish writing, and dust. They also had 256 nail and screw holes. A door to the bathroom cabinet, a ceiling fan fin, and the freezer door handle were all missing! The master bathroom floor, all mini blinds, and three window screens were damaged beyond repair. One of the kitchen cabinet doors was ripped right off its hinges. There was food spilled all over in the kitchen cabinets and the oven looked like it had not been cleaned the whole time they lived there. They had also broken off several fins on the air conditioner vents and I had to fish out a bunch of crayons that were inside. There's more, but that's the most unusual stuff.

Afzel Made My Life A Living Hell

Afzel, his wife, and their four children were from Pakistan. They moved in at the start of winter and barely lasted until spring. Right away problems began. I was told that they moved in from 11:30pm to 4am. Their neighbors started complaining about their kids running back and forth constantly, screaming loudly for long periods of time, and loud thuds. Then water began leaking from their bathroom into the apartment downstairs. I inspected everything and couldn't find a problem. I caulked everything but the problem persisted. Then I replaced the washers on the bathtub's water control valves. That didn't help either. Finally, I replaced the tub drain and the pipes leading to it. On this visit, I found the source of those loud thuds when I saw one of their children jumping off the top of a chest. It took me a little longer to do this job, so I closed the bathroom door to avoid all the racket the kids were making. As I was leaving, Afzel accused me of spying on them.

They didn't have any furniture to speak of. The living room was bare. I saw his wife and kids sitting on the floor several times. They never paid their rent on time. One month, Afzel told me they had applied for "emergency aid" but were turned down. When I took them to eviction court, he told the judge that the "emergency aid" was still pending. I pointed at him and said, "He's lying. He told me they were turned down." I was very fortunate to have an excellent judge. He told his bailiff to get their social worker on the phone. He then asked her what the status of their case was. She said they had been turned down. The judge angrily told Afzel, "You lied to this court. I grant Mr. Bangheader an immediate writ of eviction. You are out." There was never a water leakage problem in that unit after that. I now believe they were not closing the shower curtain or letting the children bathe unattended or both and lots of water was getting on the floor and leaking down through small cracks.

Absconding Appoliner

Appoliner hailed from Colombia, and he liked to go there without notifying me, or paying his rent. The first time he was MIA with no notice, I was able to reach his sister, and she paid his rent. The second time I couldn't reach her. He got back and paid the same day that I was going to court. Even when he was in town, I had to chase him around for the rent every month. I usually had to meet him somewhere on the 8th or the 10th of the month. He was always late. One month, he said he would pay me on the 4th. On the 4th, he said the 8th, on the 8th he said the 11th, on the 11th, he said the 12th, on the 12th he said the 15th. Finally, on the 19th he gave me two thirds of his rent! He said he would have the rest the next day. It came 8 days later on the 27th. Sometimes, he would have his friends call and beg me to give him a break.

He did automotive work and, even though my rental agreement prohibits doing that in my parking lot, I would frequently find all kinds of old auto parts and puddles of oil in his parking spot. His next door neighbors complained about the strong smell of marijuana coming from his unit. He always denied it. When I came to investigate, I heard a bird singing. He had gotten a parrot!

On his final trip to Colombia, while living in my building, he returned on the 15th without the rent that had been due on the 1st. I evicted him. After he moved out, I found evidence that his roommate had been toking. He had covered the entire heating vent in his room with plastic to keep the smell in.

Melanie's Malfunctions

Melanie was a single lady in her early 20s with a good job. Then she moved her boyfriend in with his large dog. Of course she didn't ask if that was OK. I found out when another resident called me and said his dog was running loose in the hallway. At first, I thought they were mistaken, since she didn't have any pets on her lease. This happened several times. Once, after I called her about it, she went around the building knocking on doors asking the other residents, "Who's talking shit about me",and she left me a nasty message saying she was getting a lawyer and breaking her lease. She said, "We're out of here!" (Melanie Mouths Off- Audio #8)

Finally, I got a call that her apartment door was wide open, the dog was running loose in the hallway, and she and her boyfriend were passed out on their living room floor naked! After a night of partying, they lost their keys and broke the door jamb to get in. That's why the door wouldn't stay closed. She also posted a two page note in the laundry room, complaining about someone stealing her detergent and how much of a F-ing loser they were. (See note, pages 180-181)

That's Pretty Fuck-ED
up when people
steal Other people's
laundry Soap My
Question is WHY the
Fuck did you leave
the BLEACH & Fabric
Softener Behind it WAS
Right with the laundry
SOAP ON the SidE OF

WASHER !! ARE
you that Fucking
much OF A LOSER!!
AND that POOR!!
you HAVE
   to STEAL FROM your
Neighbors. #6 MYOUST
   KNOCK
   ON MY
   DOOR
   thats OK youll
Get yours one way
   or another !!

Newlyweds To Dread

Salina and Darrell seemed like a nice young couple who were planning on getting married about a month after moving in. Darrell was a black man who worked at a food bank that my mother's church used to supply their homeless feeding program and community outreach. She said he was the nicest person who worked there. Salina was a Hispanic lady who worked for a temp agency. Things went fine for a few months after the wedding, and then the loud fighting started. He moved back to his parents house a few months after that. She got a roommate and, a couple of months after that, he moved back in. Then, she caught him having sex with her roommate, and all hell broke loose. Her roommate moved out and so did he. She couldn't afford the rent on her own. She even tried to convince me to put her electric bill in my name. I didn't. When the rent was due, I couldn't reach her. Then other residents started reporting a bad smell coming from her unit. A few days later someone called and said it smelled like someone was dead in there. I was afraid that, with all the drama, she might have committed suicide. That night I got drunk and went in to investigate. No dead body, but the electricity had been turned off and all the food in the refrigerator and freezer was rotting. She had moved out, leaving all of her furniture, including a huge King size bed with headboard and baseboard, lots of clothing, big TV's (not flat screens), and basically everything she owned, behind. I never heard from either one of them again.

The Players In The Big Showdown

All of the stories about my eight family building are in chronological order. Ironically, the wildest one unfolded last in early 2011. There were no guns, bats, or swords in this epic battle, but the drama between three units on the first floor was unprecedented. The players were Dick and Jane in Unit #1, Gary and Helga next door in Unit #3, and Jezebel across the hall in unit #4.

Dick, aka Diabolical Dick, was a working man who went from job to job. He was also a petty thief, and a habitual liar with a big mouth. Jane was his unemployed, stay at home girlfriend. I was skeptical when I rented to them since they had a judgment from a past landlord, but I gave them a chance. I will never forget what Dick told me,"You won't have any problems with us, Jerry." That could be considered one of the biggest lies of mankind!

Almost from the start, Dick was a tenant who was the first to complain and the last to comply. Not long after moving in, he called me claiming someone had covered his vehicle with notes that said "If you don't live here keep your junk out of our lot." He told me he was now driving a different vehicle and, if he caught the notes author, he would, "push their face in." (Diabolical Dick- Audio #10) Some of the rules he violated, and irritations he caused during his first year living in my building, included parking several inoperable vehicles in the parking lot, (including vehicles with flat tires), letting his dog run loose in the hallway, calling about every little thing, and paying the rent late most months.

I just ran into a former tenant who lived in the building at the same time Dick did. She told me that she caught Dick stealing the annual renewal sticker from her license plate. She never reported this to me at the time of the incident, presumably because she was afraid of him retaliating against her.

Helga worked and Gary was her stay at home boyfriend, who had been fired from the TSA and had been "looking for a job" for two years. He was one of those cop wanna-be, know-it-all, legal-eagle, computer geek kind of guys who had way too much free time on his hands.

Jezebel was on SSI disability and didn't qualify to rent from me because of my income requirements, but her ex sister in law, who had a good job, co-signed for her. She portrayed herself as being almost blind, and acted like her dog was a seeing- eye dog. Less than two months after moving in, she got a car and was driving around! As it turned out, her problems were more mental than physical and, once I got to know her, it seemed like she had the mentality of a 12-14 year old. Pam was a woman Jezebel illegally moved into her apartment without my knowledge.

Jezebel gave me a wrapped box of chocolates for Christmas the first year she lived in my building. That was the first time a tenant had ever done anything like that. Then she started calling early and often. She wanted a single handle kitchen faucet like Dick and Jane had. I told her I would install it for free, but she would have to pay for it since there was nothing wrong with her faucet. She said,"OK." After I did the installation, she said,"I called the tenants union and they said I don't have to pay for it." She called about a "moldy" smell on

184

her bedroom carpet. It was her dog's urine. She said her new faucet was leaking and I would have to pay for the damaged items under the sink, and claimed water was leaking from the ceiling several times. I found what appeared to be dog vomit in the spot where she claimed there was water damage. No evidence of any leaks were ever found. I had been noticing a funny odor in the vicinity of her unit. When I entered her unit to look for the source of this odor, I discovered that she had illegally moved two hamsters in.

Unfortunately, I did not keep a complete log of her phone calls, but here are the exact dates she called during a two week period in January when I did. Jan. 2: Complaint about upstairs neighbors noise, not the ones who lived above her! Jan. 4: Can she use the back door to bring in her groceries? Jan. 8: There is a "bad smell" in the hallway. She then plugged an air freshener into the hallway outlet without my permission. She was trying to cover the smell of her hamsters! Jan. 9: Can she have a key to the back door? Jan. 10: Her son was not able to get his car out of the parking lot in the middle of a snowstorm. Jan 17: Someone stole her clothes from the basement and the dryers are not working well. That's 6 calls in just 15 days and this is a fairly typical example of the barrage of calls during her first year with me. After her lease was up, I told her she would either have to move out, or sign a new rental agreement which stipulated she could only call me for serious maintenance issues or, emergencies, and no new pets. She had been driving me crazy. Can you say get a life? She had no clue how to.

Dick, Jane, Jezebel, Pam and Gary were in their 40's. Helga was in her early 30's. Jezebel's 20 year old son lived with her, and the other two units each had one minor child. Dick and

Jane befriended Jezebel when she moved in and she began watching his son at times during the day. Jezebel also befriended Gary and Helga when they moved in. It was one big happy family for awhile.

The Big Showdown

Now that you know a little bit about the players, it's show time! Somehow, some of my residents know when I am on vacation - lord knows I do not tell them- and trouble erupts. This feud turned into a molten lava flow that lasted almost a year.

Since Gary was not working, I hired him to shovel the sidewalks in the winter months. Dick told me that he had told Gary, "If you're going to shovel the walk like that you may as well not do it at all." That was not a very nice thing to say but unfortunately, it was frequently true. Gary was not going to let Dick's snide remark go without retaliating.

Soon thereafter, on a mid- March night at 11pm, while I was out of state on vacation, Gary called and said, "I was up late working on my computer when a cloud of marijuana smoke came wafting into my apartment from the unit next door," which was Dick's unit. I called Dick and he denied smoking. Two days later, Dick called claiming someone had seen Gary break out his car's tail light, but he would not reveal who his witness was.

When I returned to town, I learned that Jezebel had moved another woman in with her named Pam, who was supposedly her "caregiver",but was actually on SSI disability herself. I would learn later that she was Dick's ex-girlfriend and the mother of his son. Obviously, Dick had introduced them to each other and possibly even suggested this living arrangement. There was also a large, used couch dumped in the middle of the common area in the basement. Dick confessed that he had gotten it, thinking Pam would want it. She didn't.

I got several more calls from Gary regarding the pot smoke. Each time, I talked to Dick and he denied it. On April 15, 2011 Gary called the police with the same complaint at 10:06pm. He then woke up his girlfriend and she said she smelled it too. Dick allowed the police to search his unit and they found nothing and smelled nothing but air freshener. Four days later Gary called the police saying someone he believed to be Dick stood outside his door and said, "Someone would be hurt," and "he would knock somebody's teeth out if they didn't keep their mouth shut." The very next day, Gary called the police again, reporting that Dick said,"Enjoy your time with your daughter because I am going to beat you up." After that, Gary moved his vehicle away from the property and got an older car with fake bullet holes in the trunk area. (See picture next page)

Two days later Jezebel called the police, claiming Dick's girlfriend, Jane, had come into her apartment while she was sleeping and stolen 33 Percocet pills from a bottle containing 85 pills, and she suspected Dick and Jane were using and selling pills and marijuana. The next day, Gary called me and said, "I just wanted to let you know that Dick now has seven people living in his apartment, which is a violation of your rental agreement."

A week and a half later, I sat down to talk to Gary and Helga about the unsubstantiated calls to the police, and question Gary

about Dick's broken tail light. He immediately presented me with 8 pages of information on the harmful effects of second hand marijuana smoke and how it damages children, and information about a tenant's right to break their lease if they are living in a dangerous situation. His mother, who did not live with him and had no business being involved in this conversation, was present. Less than a minute after I began speaking she interrupted me. I pointed my finger at her and said, "You are not involved in this so don't interrupt me." Gary got up, grabbed his phone and walked out of the room. He then called the police, claiming I had, "threatened them and become aggressive." That's when I left. We were done. Any credibility he had with me was gone. A 40 something year old man, who needs his Mother to talk for him, is no man in my books. The police did not believe his claim. That was the first and last time a tenant ever called the police on me for any reason.

Even though they had two months left on their first one year lease, I gave Gary and Helga a 30 day notice to move. A few days later, I received a call from their legal aid lawyer saying I cannot give them a notice to move until their lease is over. I found that ironic, since they had just given me information about a law allowing them to break their lease if they were in a dangerous situation. They should have been glad that I had no objection to their moving. I guess what they really wanted was to stay and keep fighting.

Eleven days later, Gary reported smelling marijuana again and told the police dispatcher that he wanted the police to come into his unit first so they could smell it. When they arrived he did not answer his door but Dick answered his and allowed a full search. Nothing was found but the police reported a slight smell of marijuana in the master bathroom. The next day, Gary e-mailed Dick's employer claiming Dick was "stealing stuff." Two days later, the police 911 number received several hang up calls from Dick. Finally, at 11:14pm, he connected with the police reporting that Pam was causing a disturbance by loudly knocking on his door late at night and demanding to see her son, who she had lost custody of, and that she was refusing to leave. This disturbance was verified to me by other residents not involved in the feud. The next day, I told Jezebel that Pam,who was living there illegally, had to move out immediately. Less than a week later, Dick claimed that his son confided in him that Jezebel had touched his "Wee Wee" several times when she was watching him in the past. He then got a child abuse restraining order against her. Dick also made the claim to me that Jezebel was "blowing" Gary and another man in the building when their girlfriends were at work. Two days later, Gary called saying he heard a loud fight in the hallway, and Jezebel called saying she was afraid to go out of her apartment because Dick had threatened her. Then Gary called Child Protective Services claiming Dick was harming his daughter with clouds of marijuana smoke coming into their unit. That was impossible since the units have no direct connection. As you may have surmised, Gary, Helga, and Jezebel had teamed up against Dick and Jane. Even though Gary and Helga may have been somewhat right about the marijuana, they were trying to circumvent my authority as the building owner by calling the police, all the time, instead of me. The police do not and will not operate my property, and for that reason and their false claim to the police that I had threatened them, they had to go. When their lease was up the next month, I gave them another 30 day notice that stuck. Although he did have many bad points, Dick had lived there for two years before Gary and Helga moved in, and no one else had ever complained about him smoking marijuana.

Now the battle shifted. It was now Gary, Helga, and Jezebel against Dick, Jane, and me, and none of them were going to relinquish the fight. First, Gary called the City Building Inspector claiming all sorts of problems in his unit and the buildings common areas, and let the inspector into the basement and common areas without my knowledge. The only problems they found in the basement were a few items in a storage locker less than 24 inches from the ceiling, and improperly stored gasoline in Gary's storage locker! The only problems found in his apartment were a damaged electrical outlet and fixture that was not damaged when they moved in, and a supposedly defective oven door. That oven is still in use more than five years later. No repair was ever made and the current resident has no problem with it.

Six days later, which was just five days before she moved out, Jezebel called the City Building Inspector. I believe Gary gave her the idea. The only problem he found was a "defective privacy lock" on her lower front door lock. I had intentionally disabled these locks because so many people, or their children, were locking themselves out.

When Jezebel presented me with her notice to move, it stipulated that I must meet her at her apartment at 10pm on the last day of the month, and that, "I may not enter the apartment until she arrives!" Around this time, Jezebel's co-signer confided in me that the reason Jezebel was causing so many problems, and why I should give her a break, was because she is bipolar.

After Jezebel's departure, things quieted down a bit, but Gary and Helga still had a month left. Without backup they weren't as aggressive, but it wasn't completely over. Less than a week later, on the 4th of July, Gary called the police claiming Dick was grilling too close to the building. The building's exterior is completely concrete so a fire caused by grilling is impossible. The next morning, Gary called me and said they had no hot water. Dick was a plumber by trade. He did a few projects for me around the building. He was also the only person, other than myself, that had a key to the side of the basement where Gary's hot water heater was located. I called him and asked him to check on it. He called back and said the pilot light had gone out and he relighted it. A week later, it happened again.

This time, I went and investigated it myself. I found that Dick had turned their water temperature down all the way. He was expecting another call from me, and being paid a few bucks for "helping me out." Instead, I caught him red handed. Of course he denied it, claiming someone else must have a key. No one else did. I had just changed the lock recently and he was the only person I gave a key to. He must have thought it was pretty funny for Gary and Helga to wake up and have to take a cold shower. I never told them the real reason their hot water was cold. On July 23, Gary called the police claiming Dick had followed him to a parking lot about a mile away from the building and threatened him. No specific threat was mentioned. Soon thereafter, Gary and Helga took Dick to court and got a two year restraining order against him. Just a few days after that, Gary and Helga moved out.

That same day, I got a letter from the State Department of Consumer Affairs stating Jezebel had filed a complaint against me. One of the questions on the form she supposedly filled out asked, "Please describe your complaint." This was the answer given, "Harassment, discrimination against the disabled, not fixing already broken items, ceiling in bathroom caving in, already damaged carpeting, door that didn't lock, broken refrigerator that was never fixed, damaged kitchen floor and ceiling leaking in living room and master bedroom." This complaint was filed online. Since I knew Jezebel did not own or use a computer, and everything stated was false, the complaint did not ring true to me. I called her co- signer and asked if she knew anything about it. She said,"No" and that she would call Jezebel and ask her about it. Jezebel told her that she had not filed this complaint. I then asked The Department of Consumer Affairs to investigate and find the source of this fraudulent claim against me. They told me, "We don't do that." I figured out that either Jezebel's son, or Gary and Helga, or all three, collaborating together, had done it. They were the only ones with enough information (such as Jezebel's new address which I didn't even have) to do it. Jezebel's son had given me an ear full one day in the hallway saying how I had mistreated his mom, and falsely accused her of not picking up behind her dog. I believe I was the one who was deceived and mistreated by all the players involved. After Jezebel moved out, she told on herself... no more dog poop on the lawn! In the entire time she lived there, I did not see her pick up behind her dog once.

Five out of seven of the trouble makers were now gone. All of these problems over the smell of marijuana, and Dick not tending to his own business. I knew Dick had been smoking because I smelled it myself. If he just would have stopped or done it outside of the building, and kept his snide comments to himself, all of this trouble might have been avoided.

Gary and Helga would not give me their new address to send their security deposit back, because they said, since I knew Dick, I was a party to the restraining order. They instructed me to send it to the Postmaster. When the Postmaster was on vacation and they did not receive it in the required amount of time they called saying their attorney was going to sue me. He didn't!

As outlined in my rental agreement, I charged Jezebel for moving in an adult who was not on her lease. Her co-signer had her lawyer friend send me a letter with a small check enclosed as "final payment" and threatened to sue me stating, "If for some reason you decide to move forward with any form of litigation I believe Jezebel has a strong counterclaim of discrimination based upon her medical condition." I ended up settling with them without litigation for less than they owed, but much more than the check the lawyer sent.

Dick later admitted to me that he had put oil in the gas tank of Gary's snow blower before Gary moved out. Almost seven months after Gary and Helga moved out, there was an anonymous call to the DARE hotline alleging drug use and sales in Dick and Jane's apartment. The police responded and found no evidence of either. I am quite sure who made that call. That was probably the day Gary found out his snow blower had been vandalized.

All told, during this battle, there were 15 calls to the police, two restraining orders issued, two reports of child abuse to social services, five alleged threats of physical violence, three known and one alleged act of vandalism and tampering, a report of improper sexual conduct involving three adults, two calls requesting apartment inspections, and false allegations of unsafe living conditions to the City Building Inspector, one e-mail claiming theft from an employer, one claim of theft from an apartment, and one fraudulent complaint against me to the State.

She's Back!
All was quiet for over a year. Then, one day, Dick confronted me in the basement demanding that I let Pam move back into the building with him and his girlfriend this time. Yes, that's the same Pam he had called the police on when she was living with Jezebel! He said if I said no, he would call the Building Inspector on me! He had lost his job and this was the only way

he could afford to stay. I said, "absolutely not." He called me later to apologize for threatening me. He said Pam was now on medication and assured me that there would be no problems. I said I would think about it.

Not wanting to have a vacancy in the middle of the winter I reluctantly agreed to it. Everything was quiet for a few months and then Pam started calling the police. First, several hang ups to 911, and then reporting that she left her phone with a former boyfriend and he would not return it. Then, a report that her "friend" stole her pain medication and food stamp card. Five days later, her uncle called the police saying Pam called him and said her live in boyfriend was putting his hands on her. I am not sure who that could have been since no other man was living with them and, as far as I knew, Dick was not her boyfriend. Thank God, Dick got a job and Pam moved out. Afterwards, Dick confided in me that he was very happy about this, stating, "She was driving me crazy."

Around the time that she moved out, I noticed a small dorm refrigerator that I had in my storage locker was missing. My locker was located in a part of the basement that only Dick and I had a key to, and he was the only one who knew where I hid the key to that locker. I had told him where the key was so he could access some extra plumbing parts if I hired him to do a repair. When I asked him about the missing refrigerator, he said he knew nothing about it. A week later, it was returned to the locker. He claimed Pam had taken it with her, mistakenly. Since she was not authorized to enter that part of the basement, and did not have a key or know where my locker key was hidden, his story seemed very unlikely. I didn't make a big deal about it since I got it back.

Wait, There's More

Less than two years, later Dick moved out. Although he didn't cause any more "major" problems, other than the many obnoxious voice mails he left me, there were a lot of little irritations he brought my way almost every week during this time period. On one of those occasions, when I arrived at the property, I caught him parking completely in someone else's spot. When I confronted him, he said, "Blow Me." That's when I said, "Don't raise your voice to me, chump." He then left me three nasty messages. (Audio #11-13) In message #11, he claimed he was fifty two, when he was actually forty eight, and in message #13, he claimed that his lease entitled him to two parking spaces, when in fact it did not guarantee him any.

Soon thereafter, he told me he would not be home when I came to pick up the rent, and that I should enter his apartment and get the rent from the kitchen table. An hour later, he called back accusing his new neighbor of smoking pot. He said, "I smelled pot in the hallway, and when I saw him in the hallway he was baked." (Audio #14) I found out later that he was just trying to cover his own tracks, since he had told me to enter his apartment.

The door would be left unlocked, the lights would be left on frequently, and small things of mine would disappear every few months from the side of the basement that only he and I had a key to. First, it was a paint brush and a putty knife, then a metal drink bottle, then an 8' section of copper pipe. I did not mention the smaller things, but when the pipe disappeared I did. He said the boy working for him must have taken it accidentally. Funny thing was, I never saw anyone working for him. He then replaced it.

I require all pets to be leashed while in the common areas of the building. Even after speaking with her about it several times, I still found Dick's girlfriend taking their dog out with no leash a number of times. I did not confront them about this because I was just too sick and tired of always having to talk to them about problems which they caused, and their frequent belligerent responses.

Once, when I was visiting the building I saw him pull up to the back door and honk his horn so his girlfriend would come out. I had informed him, previously, that I do not permit that type of behavior. He also knew that the back door was only to be used for emergencies and moving, but I found it intentionally left unlatched on a number of occasions, and believed he was responsible. He told on himself when he moved out. After his departure, I didn't find that door left open for quite a long time.

On several other occasions, I got calls from other residents complaining about his vehicle taking up more than one parking space. They couldn't get into their parking spots which caused me to come to the property late in the evening to investigate. (Audio #15)

Dick's Last Stand

Many times when I confronted Dick about something he was doing wrong he would say, "I'm in my 50s. I'm too old to do things like that." When he actually turned 50, almost two years after he started claiming he was, I sent him a letter outlining many of the problems he had caused, warning him that even one more small problem would result in me terminating his tenancy and stating, "Now that you are actually going to be 50, I expect you to act like it."

Dear Dick,

Happy Birthday! You have been telling me for years that you are in your fifties. In fact, I kept the recording of a message you left me over a year ago claiming you were fifty two. Now that you are actually going to be 50, at least if the date of birth in your computer records and on the rental application you gave me are correct, I expect you to act like it.

When you moved in, I was a bit skeptical, since you had a judgment from a past landlord, but I gave you a chance. I will never forget what you told me then. You said "You won't have any problems with us, Jerry." Well, I have had many, many, many problems with you and, unlike any tenant I have had before or since, you have had problems with many of your neighbors. You manipulated Jezebel into moving Pam into her apartment without my knowledge. She went on to make a scene in the hallway by banging on your door demanding to see her son and causing the police to come to the building. You would not stop smoking pot in the building even after I talked to you about it many times, and the police came several times. You tampered with Gary's hot water heater twice, causing me to come to the building. When I caught you red handed, you claimed someone else must have a key. Well, no one else did. If you really believed that someone did, you would not have left all your tools out in plain sight just one week after that incident. Why would someone come in there and just turn the control on one hot water heater down? They wouldn't. Those are just a few of the major problems you have caused me.

In the last year, you caused me to come to the building late at night because you parked in two spots and someone had no place to park. When I called you about it the next day, you got loud and left me three very nasty messages. You dumped multiple items in the common area of the building, including a couch, a bicycle, and the contents of your storage locker in the basement. When I saw you in the basement, you said you were putting the things back in your locker. Two hours later, I came down to the basement and everything was still out. That's when I threw it all back in your locker myself. I called you and ask you to pump up the tires on Jim's truck, which you claimed now belonged to you. Three days later, when I came over, the tires were still flat. You then came running out with your air compressor. Too late then. On two separate recent occasions, you left tools and plumbing materials on the rear stairway landing, where someone could easily trip over them. You honked your horn in the back of the building so your girlfriend would come out. This is something that you complained to me about when someone else did it. You know I don't allow this, yet you did it right in front of me. You falsely accused several of your neighbors of smoking pot to try and cover your trail including, most recently, claiming your new neighbor was "baked." For your information, they both get drug tested and do not smoke pot. On many occasions in the last year, I have heard you screaming loud profanities in your apartment. One time, I could hear it all the way in the basement.

You told me that you had taken an Anger Management course, but if you really did, it did not work. If you didn't, you should. I think it would do you and everyone around you a lot of good.

Since you moved in, you have generated 16 police calls to the building, including your neighbors complaining about you. That is totally unacceptable. You demanded that I let Pam move back in and assured me that there would be no problems and the rent would be paid on time. In the time she lived there last year, the full rent was paid on time only once, and she generated 6 police calls to the building. Yes, I just went and got the records and now I know exactly what was going on. Not even close to what you promised me.

On top of all this, you still pay your rent late most months.

Just a few months ago, you knew I was coming between 6:30 and 7pm to collect the rent. You called me and said you would be there by 7:30pm. You showed up at 8pm and, then, only had $300.00 That is abuse. I do not collect rent on your schedule. The next time that happens, I will be leaving if you do not show up when I tell you I will be there, and the full late fee will apply.

Just like you, I am getting older and less patient with people who give me headaches. I work hard to be a good landlord. I have given you many breaks and even given you work in the building whenever I could. Your rent does not include me picking up behind you, being your therapist, or dealing with unnecessary problems. **If you cannot stop causing problems, big or small, I will be giving you a notice to move.** If the door to our side of the basement is left unlocked one more time, you will have to remove your things and use a regular locker like everyone else. If I find any item of yours left in any common area of the building, your vehicle irregularly parked, or you violating any other rule in your rental agreement, you will immediately be assessed the full penalty as outlined in your rental agreement. I have already given you way too many breaks. In case you do not have a copy anymore, I have enclosed all three pages for you to review. Read it over carefully, because "I didn't know" will not be an acceptable excuse for any violation.

I know this is not the most pleasant birthday letter, but you have caused unnecessary unpleasantness in my life many, many, many times over the last few years, and I just want to be clear with you that either that is going to completely change or you will no longer be welcome to live at my property. I do believe you can make the right choices, and I hope, for your sake, that you do. If you choose to make both of our lives easier, I will not raise your rent again unless my operating costs increase significantly.

After receiving this letter, he had a knee jerk reaction, blowing up and leaving me five very nasty messages that same day. (Audio #16-20) He didn't follow through on any of the threats he made in these messages nor did he become my "aspirin" as he stated he would, by moving out.

I require my tenants to comply with State and Local laws on my property. One of those laws is to have valid license plates on your vehicles in the parking lot. Less than a month before moving out, one of his vehicles had no plates. I spoke with him about it. The next day, when I came, he had moved the plates from one of his vehicles to another. Still no plates on one of his vehicles; just a different vehicle!

Not long before moving out, he said one of his faucets was leaking and he had replaced a washer fixing it. I paid him $20.00 for doing this repair. When he moved out, it was still leaking. I checked and he had not replaced any parts. That was just one job I paid him for that wasn't done. There were a number of other jobs he claimed to have done and was paid for that I now believe he made up or didn't do right. When he moved out, I also found two toilet stoppers in his unit which he had replaced. They were the wrong size, causing water to leak, which ran up my water bill. He also, frequently, littered green bottle caps, used plumbing parts, and parts that had fallen off of his vehicles in the parking lot.

A few days before moving out, Dick told me that he was going to take an anger management course. I guess he forgot that he had already told me he had taken one.

A day after he moved out, he called demanding his security deposit back right away. The law gives me 21 days to return what he had coming. To avoid any more hassles with him, I returned it a few days later only to find additional damage in his unit afterwards. My phone has been much quieter and my life is a lot more peaceful since he departed.

Epilogue
Some of the names, and voices were changed to protect the guilty, high maintenance, disturbed, and inconsiderate tenants. They should be exposed so other landlords know what they are up against before deciding if they will rent to them.

Landlords should not be required to clean up tenants messes, remove their furniture, be contacted by municipalities threatening to turn their property into a nuisance property because of tenants actions, or deal with a multitude of other problems which should require a maid, social worker, moving company, psychotherapist, arbitrator, loan officer, collection agency, or punching bag subject to their loud and profane verbal abuse when they screw up and you call them on it. They get in a brawl, I get a call! If things don't get better, I get a letter from the city, or police, or both.

Their rent did not even come close to covering all the unnecessary grief and mental aggravation they gave me, nor should I be expected to endure it as a "cost of doing business." If they gave me a piece of their mind in the form of a verbally abusive phone message, I kept it and now I'm sharing those pieces with the world.

These are just the most dramatic experiences I have had in the last 20 years as a landlord. There have been many incidents when I had to speak with tenants about following the rules outlined in their rental agreement, most notably moving unauthorized pets and roommates in, not picking up after their pets go to the bathroom, parking improperly, having too many vehicles in the parking lot, and not paying their rent on time. My rental agreement has grown with my experiences. It's up from one page to three.

After reading these horror stories, who would want to be a landlord? Well, as of this writing, I'm still in the business! I guess you either must have crocodile skin, or develop it to survive. They say what doesn't kill you will make you stronger, and I believe, after 20 years, I am...wiser too.

If you are reading this book purely for its entertainment value, you can skip "You Early Retire". It is the only part of this book that is specifically written to help educate those interested in getting into real estate, or help improve the skills of those who already are.

After revealing so many bad things that can happen, it would only be fair to balanced journalism to discuss the positive aspects of the real estate business and how those who are interested can achieve financial independence. Since enhancing my screening process, my business has run a lot more smoothly. Yes, there are still some occasional minor irritations and it takes a little longer to get a unit rented but there have not been any problems that come close to the stories in "Baptized By Fire."

There are always new firsts in this business. Just last week, I was threatened by an applicant who I turned down because he lied on his rental application. He did not take too kindly to my screening process. (Audio #21) He said he had lived at his current residence for two years, but I found out that he had been living at another address just six months earlier and his previous address was a jail called the House Of Correction! Forty years old with a fresh battery conviction. Just the kind of tenant I'm looking for-Not!

Landlord Stories- You Early Retire

There are many ways to become rich and financially independent. You could inherit a lot of money, marry a wealthy person, make a wise or lucky investment in the stock market, get a large insurance settlement, invent something wanted or needed by the masses, find a large sum of money or jewels, start your own successful company, become a professional athlete, entertainer, artist, or actor, buy that lucky lottery ticket, or hit a big jackpot at a casino.

Unfortunately, the vast majority of people will never become wealthy or financially independent using any of those methods. With the uncertainty of the stock market, the volatility of the bond market, the low yield of savings accounts and CDs, and the high risk, long working hours, and investment of starting your own business, I believe there is a much better way… real estate.

Before I got into the real estate business, I read many books on the subject. Some had a few good ideas, but many were filled with pie in the sky exaggerated claims of getting rich quickly by buying foreclosed properties or making "no money down" deals. Some people do make money this way, if they really know what they are doing.

My method is a lot safer and surer. This chapter will teach you the practical realities of being a successful landlord.

A number of my personal friends who are in the business call on me for advice. Now I will share everything I have learned about the rental business with you.

I bought my first rental property when I was 37 years old. Now twenty years later, I am semi-retired, having paid off my property in less than 15 years. I make 35-40 thousand dollars a year, and work an average of five hours a week. That includes time spent doing management duties like cutting the grass, shoveling snow, vacuuming and cleaning the common areas, pulling weeds, fixing up units when someone moves out, and whatever else is needed to keep the property operating well and looking good. I haven't been able to find a manager who performs at the level I demand, so I do it myself. My income represents a whopping 50-55% annual return on the initial down payment I made on this property.

Through all of the hardships, I would never trade it for having to work for someone else. I am my own boss and, other than a rare emergency, I work when I choose. In 20 years, I have never received an emergency call in the middle of the night. If a tenant doesn't like something, they can move out at the end of their lease, and if I don't like something about them, I can order them to move. I am not going anywhere. If the stock market and/or economy crashes, my property will still be standing and people will still need a place to live.

Saving isn't always easy, but if you weren't born rich it is necessary to create wealth and financial freedom. This requires living below your means, and having a monthly budget which includes money set aside for saving. Set goals and make a spreadsheet outlining how to reach them. Instead of putting money in a retirement account, put it in a regular savings account so it is available, without penalty, when needed for investing in real estate. That new boat, motorcycle, fancy clothing, electronic gadget, or other expensive toys may have to wait. Let's face it, they probably won't get used that much anyway.

New vehicles are a very poor investment. Many people feel they need or deserve a new vehicle. The fact of the matter is, unless it is a rare model, it will never appreciate in value; insurance and purchase costs are higher than a used vehicle, and that first scratch or dent hurts a lot more! Leasing a vehicle is just as bad. I recently bought a used car in great condition that was only six years old for just 25% of the price it sold for new. Save and pay cash for a used vehicle. By doing this, you can avoid the cost of comprehensive insurance and just carry liability insurance. There are no interest payments on a loan either. As your net worth increases, you should increase the amount of liability coverage on your auto policy. Always have a mechanic you trust check the vehicle out before buying it.

You must separate your wants from your needs. Make your own coffee and save $500-$1000 a year, Don't equate your self worth with the "things" you own, do it with your "Net Worth," which is the value of your valuable assets minus all debts.

Never ever carry credit card debt. If you have a balance now, pay it off as quickly as possible and don't add anything else to it. Transfer current balances to a new card that offers free interest on balance transfers. Credit cards are very handy to have if you need to rent a car or just don't like carrying cash. Use them the right way by paying your full balance each month and getting one that pays you cash rewards. Pay off any other consumer debt as quickly as possible. Anytime you pay interest for something you thought you had to have right now, you are giving away money that you can never get back.

Unlike real estate loans, the government does not allow you to deduct the interest on consumer loans on your income taxes.

Paying your credit card bill and all of your other bills, on time, every month, is the very best way to build a great credit rating which helps you get the best interest rates when you are ready to buy a property. Having only a few credit cards also improves your credit rating.

Just because you need to save doesn't mean you can't treat yourself to something nice, see a show or concert, or take a vacation. Just do these things when you have the money to pay for them, and try not to be too extravagant. I have found that traveling by automobile on vacation is much more affordable than flying. You can bring a lot more things with you and, if you bring most of your own food, it is much cheaper and can be a lot healthier than eating out. Up until a few years ago, most of my vacations involved some camping-very affordable. Going to places like Florida in the off season is much more affordable. I like to go in November. It is getting much colder in the north where I live, yet the hotel rates are 30-50% less than in March.

If you have a like- minded partner, it is much easier to reach your goals. My wife and I were both good savers. The same year we met, we bought a nice, yet modest home. We each put 20% of its cost down. After examining an amortization chart, I realized that if we each put an extra $200.00 a month toward the mortgage, it would be paid in full in just under five years. The interest charged on a loan is more than the interest a bank will pay you for money in your savings account, so paying off your mortgage early is a win-win. After paying our home off, we used the money we would have been putting into that payment to save for a rental property. Some people start out buying a duplex and live in one of the units to build equity. If this works for you, there is nothing wrong with it. All the duplexes we looked at were more expensive to buy, per unit, than a four family building or larger. The property taxes were also higher, due to its higher value. Personally, I do not want to live with my tenants. I don't want to know about all of their day to day business, and I don't want them knowing about all of mine.

We found a four family building we liked in the "for sale by owner" section of our local newspaper, and got a conventional loan. That is a loan in which you put a minimum of 20% down and it is amortized over 15-30 years with a fixed interest rate. Get a mortgage with no prepayment penalty. Unless you have some kind of windfall, or a much larger savings account than most people, and can afford to pay more than 20% down, or cash for the entire property, this is the only way I recommend buying a rental property. If you borrow more than 80% of the money needed to purchase the property, you are over-leveraged and face a much greater chance of defaulting. As I mentioned in Baptized By Fire, the man who bought my four family building was foreclosed on in just 13 months because he was over leveraged. Never fall into this trap.

Work with a bank to get a pre-approved line of credit so you know what your interest rate will be and how much you are qualified to borrow. If you are pre-approved, you can act quickly and close the deal when you find the right property. Good properties usually get snatched up in a hurry.

Once you buy a property, keep an eye on interest rates. If they drop one half percent or more, you may be able to lower your payments, or increase the amount you are paying toward your mortgage monthly by refinancing. Always add in the costs of closing before refinancing, and be sure that those costs don't outweigh the benefits. When the rates dropped, we refinanced with the same company our mortgage was already with.

Have at least $1000.00 per unit in savings, in case you run into any financial speed bumps like an unexpected large repair, or a long vacancy. If your savings are greater than this amount, I recommend putting the excess toward paying off your mortgage. No other investment will give you as good of a return as you will receive from reducing your debt which is guaranteed.

There are many niche markets in investment property. I have some friends and acquaintances who have invested in these areas and they have done quite well. If you know someone who invests in these markets and it interests you, try to learn all that you can from them. I do not flip houses, build spec houses, invest in inner city properties or foreclosures, which can be had on the cheap but are usually a lot of work and headaches, or invest in single family homes, which can be very low maintenance.

 My area of expertise is multi-family buildings, specifically, a four family and an eight family. With a larger group of tenants, you have more cash flow so you can use "opm" (other people's money) to pay off your property sooner.

My experiences have taught me to do a lot of research before renting to anyone. I now tell perspective tenants, when they call, that I pre-screen everyone so I don't waste anyone's time. I require a minimum household income of thirty thousand dollars a year, and a minimum of two years at their current employer, and two years at their current rental, or any combination of those two that add up to four years. Then I ask them if they would qualify under those terms. This way I don't waste my time showing the place to someone I would not rent to.

Screen your rental applicants online. Checking their credit history, evictions, criminal records, and the sex offender registry is a must. Their job and rental history are also very important. Check all references thoroughly. I even go as far as verifying that the person they say is their landlord, actually owns the property they live in through public records. Some people will give you the phone number of a friend or relative claiming they are their landlord. When calling their landlord, don't divulge the information they gave you. Instead, ask how long have they been living at this property, how much their rent is, what the address of the property where they live is, where they work, and do they have any pets. Also, ask if they have been good tenants, did they pay their rent on time, have you had any problems with them, did they give you proper notice that they were moving, why are they moving, and would you rent to them again. Make sure the information their landlord and employer give you matches what they put on their application. Verify that the phone number they gave you for their employer is actually the number of that company. You can never guarantee how someone will behave, but past performance is frequently indicative of future behavior. Ask to see their ID so you know they really are who they say they are. Does the address and birth date on their ID match what they put on their rental application?

Some warning signs that someone might not be the best person to rent to include people who call you from "private" or "unavailable" phone numbers, those who mark their message to you "urgent", people who start telling you how nice the apartment is when they are barely in the door, start planning where they will put their furniture, say, "God bless you" on the phone or after submitting an application, people who are currently living in a motel, and those who say they need to move in as soon as possible.

I give all new tenants the following speech: "I am a good landlord and, if you have a problem, let me know right away because I like to fix little problems before they become big ones. I am strict with the rent and, if you don't pay your rent when it is due, I will be giving you a 5 day notice to pay or move. If you don't pay or move out after that, I will be taking you to court, because if you don't have the rent this month, it is very unlikely that you will have twice that amount next month, and I am running a business not a charity."

Be and do everything you espouse. That is how you build credibility and respect. I also instruct new tenants to be friendly, but not to become friends with their neighbors because someone borrows something and doesn't return it, someone breaks something belonging to someone else and doesn't replace it, or someone looks at someone else's significant other the wrong way and trouble begins.

Many of the conflicts I wrote about in Baptized By Fire arose out of "friendships."

I once met another landlord while waiting in line to file an eviction at the courthouse. He said "They haven't paid me in six months and I thought I should do something." That's six months' worth of rent that he will never see. You have to act quickly, because the wheels of justice do turn slowly. If they don't pay, you must take the right steps to have them out before the end of that month. Learn the exact steps of the eviction process. You must follow them, quickly and correctly, if you don't want to lose more than the current month's rent. If you want to have a "heart", do some volunteer work or donate to a charity. Giving tenants a "break"is a sign of weakness, and if they sense this, many of them will try to take advantage of you.

Get all available material from your State, City, or Town and County on their laws regarding landlords and tenants. Study them thoroughly before getting into the business. Knowing these laws and following them can prevent costly lawsuits and trouble with government agencies if your tenant gets nasty. The vast majority of tenants do not know these laws so your knowledge and obedience of them will almost always give you the upper hand. Study and follow the federal discrimination laws also. Some of these laws change frequently, so be sure to keep up with all the latest revisions and additions to them.

If your rental property was built before 1978, you must inform your tenants and prospective tenants that there is the possibility that lead paint is present, and offer them a brochure describing the hazards and ways to prevent exposure. You must also have all new tenants sign a "Disclosure of Information on Lead-

Based Paint and/or Lead-Based Paint Hazard" form. These brochures and forms, along with all the other legal forms needed to run your rental business, can be found at your local Legal Blank Form store or online.

Know the property you are buying. Park nearby for several hours and be observant. Is there a loud factory or freeway nearby, any gang activity or drug sales, low flying planes or any other negative factors in the neighborhood? Talk to the tenants if you can. Find out if they are happy with the place they live, plan on staying, how much their rent is, and if they are aware of any major maintenance or other problems at the property. You can also evaluate what you think of them. Check with the building inspector to see if there has been any recent uncorrected violations or problems. In some places, you can also check with the police department to see if there have been any problems requiring them to respond to the property.

Many things at a property can be fixed fairly inexpensively, like hot water heaters, but it is very important to be sure major mechanicals like furnaces or boilers are in good condition. The other two most important things to check are the foundation and the roof. These can both be very expensive to repair. If they are not in good repair, and you are set on buying the property, be sure provisions are made in your offer to purchase that cover the costs of these repairs. If there are or have been any problems with the roof or foundation, check thoroughly for mold. Cleaning it up can be very costly. Always make the results of an inspection, a contingency of your offer to purchase, and have a reputable inspector do the inspection before buying a property.

If you are handy, you can save a lot of money by doing most of your own repairs. If you are not, learn to be, like I did. This could mean the difference between turning a profit or not. If you do hire someone, watch what they are doing carefully, and the next time do it yourself. The first time I had a leaky faucet, I paid a plumber $80.00 to replace a 25cent washer in ten minutes. I watched and learned. Now I do it myself. Learn how to use a power snake to clean out clogged drains and toilets. It is inexpensive to rent and, just like everything else, easy to operate once you know how. Many large home improvement stores have classes on installing carpeting, flooring, plumbing fixtures, and various other things. Some of these classes are free.

When a unit is vacant, fix it up so it looks as good as possible and check all plumbing fixtures closely. If there is a corroded shut off valve under a sink or by the toilet, replace it. Never use plastic water supply lines. If they are present, replace them with braided metal ones. I learned my lesson the hard way when one broke. No one was home and water leaked to the unit below, damaging the ceiling. Preventive maintenance is crucial if you want to avoid emergency calls and major damage. The better your property looks and is maintained, the more you can charge for rent, and you will attract better tenants that will stay longer. Never think you are too good to bend over and pick up some litter or do any job that keeps your property looking great and operating well.

If you have purchased this book yourself, or received it as a gift, you have my permission to use any or all of my rental agreement. It was designed for my multifamily properties.

Customize it to meet your needs using all of the rules that could apply to your property.

You make money in three ways with real estate: Using other people's money to pay for most of your property, depreciation, and appreciation. Let's look at these.

If you are considering buying a property, make sure the current owner or real estate agent supplies you with a list of all current operating expenses including supplies, repairs, maintenance, water, garbage and recycling collection, gas, electricity, insurance, vacancy rate, advertising, and property taxes. You also need a list of all income the property generates. Calculate your monthly payment for the property you want to buy with an amortization chart. With all of this information, you can determine if the rental income would pay all of the expenses and mortgage with at least a 5% a year return on your down payment. If all these numbers work, it should be a property that will be mostly paid for with "other people's money", also known as rent.

If you have ever heard the expression "paper losses", it describes a rental property's depreciation write off. Even though your property should increase in value over time, the government allows you to take a "depreciation" write off. This decreases your taxable income, and in some cases, may even put you in a lower tax bracket. You must take this write off, because when you sell the property, you will have to pay capital gains taxes on it, whether you took it or not. The four and eight family properties I owned had a 27 and a half year depreciation schedule. This meant I could take 80% of the purchase price or established value and divide it by 27 and a half. This was the amount that was subtracted from my income each year… a paper loss. Let's say your write off is $10,000.00 a year. When you sell this property, you pay the capital gains tax at its current rate. For example, if you owned the property for 10 years, your total write off was $100,000.00. If the capital gains tax rate at the time of sale is 20%, you would pay $20,000.00 in taxes. Be prepared, because the government takes this payment at closing on the closing date. Some states also have their own capital gains tax. The only way to avoid paying the federal capital gains tax upon its sale is to buy a like property, as defined by the IRS, in a short period of time and do a 1031 exchange or "Starker exchange" as they are commonly called.

I recommend only buying property in middle class areas or better, twenty five miles or less away from where you live. As I discussed earlier, be sure to study the property and neighborhood before investing. A good location should appreciate 3% - 7% a year. You make money not only on your down payment, but all the money the bank loaned you, too. Yes that's 3%- 7% of the full value of the property. Over time, this appreciation can add up considerably. Keeping your property in good condition should increase the potential for this appreciation.

As you can see, the income a property generates greatly increases after it is paid off. Even before that happened, the return on our down payment was almost 9% a year. This building cost us $363,400.00 to buy. At closing, the buyer gets credit for all the tenants security deposits which are taken off of your down payment, so instead of having to put $72,680.00 down, we only had to put $68,009.00 down.

The list of expenses on this page does not include deductions the government gives you on your taxes for expenses such as depreciation, legal costs, work clothing, business related meals and entertainment (within reason), and automobile mileage, which are also financial benefits afforded a landlord*. Always keep good records by maintaining a spreadsheet to chart your monthly income and expenses. *Allowable deductions are subject to change.

Expenses and Income For My Eight Family Building

	2008	2012
Advertising	1,078.	291.
Insurance	1,695.	1,889.
Garbage Collection	758.	1,393.
Utilities- Water, Gas & Electric	3,518.	4,685.
Property Taxes	12,245	13,155.
Supplies, Maintenance & Repairs	3,027.	2,741.
Mortgage Payments	26,604.	-0-
Total Expenses	48,925.	24,154.
Total Rents Collected	54,965.	60,097.
Net Profit	6,040.	35,943.

Examine my offer to purchase closely. It will give you a road map of contingencies that should be included in every offer to purchase. My closing statement will give you some insights into what expenses are typically paid for by the buyer and seller at closing. As a buyer, I recommend having a lawyer who is experienced in real estate closings present at your closing to be sure all of the legal mumbo jumbo (aka fine print) is correct.

Now that you know the basic principles of being a landlord and buying a profitable property, use them. With a willingness to work hard at times, and follow the principles I have outlined here, you can be successful. Not everyone is cut out for this type of business, but those who are will reap the benefits.

You may access and download my Rental Agreement, Closing Statement and Offer To Purchase by going to bangheader.com, clicking on the "You Early Retire" link, and entering code # uretire2

Jerry Bangheader makes no claim to the rights nor holds a copyright on any of the quips, quotes, lyrics, or sayings contained herein on pages 220-227 which starts below this disclaimer.

Favorite Rock Star and Celebrity Quips & Quotes

1. Oprah - "When I Was Making $22,000 A Year People Always Needed $50. Then When I Started Making $50,000 A Year Everybody Needed $500. Now Nobody Needs Less Than $50,000."

2. Robert Herjavec- "Don't Mistake My Kindness For Weakness."

3. Billy Joel concert quips: "The 20 Year Old Man Who Wrote These Songs Wasn't Thinking About The 50 Year Old Man Who Would Have To Sing Them", "I Don't Know Who I Feel More Sorry For, The People In The Front Who Have To Look At My Wrinkled Face or The People Behind Me Who Have To Look At My Ass", referring to his bald head, and "Billy Couldn't Make It Tonight - I'm His Dad!"

4. In a televised interview, the interviewer asked Keith Richards, "Mick runs and works out a lot what do you do to stay in shape?" Keith's response, "I Play Guitar With The Rolling Stones, That's Work Out Enough!"

5. Hugh Hefner- "My Age May Have Changed But My Taste In Women Has Not."

6. Andy Warhol- "God Gave Man A Brain And A Penis But Only Enough Blood To Operate One At A Time."

7. Charlie Sheen - "You've Got A Drug Addict, A Pot Head, And A Porn Star. What More Do You Need?" -Referring to the three women he was living with at the time.

8 & 9. Ted Nugent- "If It's Too Loud You're Too Old." & "If Anyone Wants To Get Mellow They Can Turn Around And Get The Fuck Out Of Here."

Favorite Lyrics By Others

1. Imagine All The People Living Life In Peace, You May Say I'm A Dreamer But I'm Not The Only One, I Hope Someday You'll Join Us And The World Will Be As One- John Lennon

2. Come On People Now Smile On Your Brother Everybody Get Together Try To Love One Another Right Now- Chet Powers

3. No Stems, No Seeds That You Don't Need- Acapulco Gold Is Badass Weed- Cheech & Chong

4. What's So Funny About Peace, Love, And Understanding- Nick Lowe

5. Keep Your Eyes On The Road And Your Hand Upon The Wheel- Jim Morrison

6. The World Is Full Of Kings And Queens Who Blind Your Eyes Then Steal Your Dreams- Ronnie James Dio

7. Shit, Goddamn, Get Off Your Ass And Jam- George Clinton

8. Free Your Mind And Your Ass Will Follow- George Clinton, Edward Hazel, and Raymond Davis

9. No Shoes, No Shirt, No Problem- Casey M. Beathard

10. Legalize It, Don't Criticize It- Peter Tosh

Favorite Saying and Quotes By Others

1. Rodney King after a video of him being beaten by some L.A. policemen was televised, the police officers who beat him were acquitted, and mass rioting broke out in the Los Angeles area. - "Can't We All Get Along."

2. There Are Only Three Kinds of People: People That Wish Things Would Happen, People That Make Things Happen, And People That Wonder What Happened. - Mary Kay Ash

3. I've Been Called Worse Things By Better People- Pierre Trudeau.

4. Little People Talk About Things, Middle People Talk About People, And Big People Talk About Ideas.

5. Who Died And Left You In Charge.

6. When The Going Gets Tough, The Tough Get Going. - Frank Leahy

7. Smile And The World Smiles With You, Cry And You Cry Alone. - Stanley Gordon West

8. There Are Three Sides To Every Story: Your Side, My Side, And The Truth.

9. What Comes Around Goes Around.

10. You're Young, Dumb, And Full Of Cum. - Rick King & W. Peter Iliff

11. You Can Marry More Money In 5 Minutes Than You Can Make In A Lifetime.- Richard Crouch

12. The Definition Of Stupidity: Repeating The Same Action And Expecting A Different Result.- Albert Einstein

13. Even A Man On A Diet Can Look At The Menu.

14. Loose Lips Sink Ships. - WWII Poster used to discourage people from talking about war secrets. – I always thought of the meaning more in the context of if I kiss a lady or she kisses me anything can happen!

15. Up With Shirts, Down With Pants. - Edwin Edwards

16. If You Can't Dazzle Them With Brilliance Baffle Them With Bullshit. - W.C. Fields

17. Winners Never Quit And Quitters Never Win. - Vince Lombardi

18. Ashes To Ashes, Dust To Dust, If It Weren't For You Women, Our Peckers Would Rust.

19. We've Got Too Many Chiefs And Not Enough Indians. - Dean Martin

20. You're A Vamp, A Tramp, And A Bit Of A Scamp.

21. If It Seems Too Good To Be True, It Probably Is.

22. Be Rich, Act Poor.

23. Empty Vessels Rattle The Most.

24. Things (or People) That Are In Motion Tend To Stay In Motion. Things That Are Stopped Tend To Stay Stopped.

25. An Ounce Of Prevention Is Worth A Pound Of Cure.- Ben Franklin

26. Think Globally Act Locally.

27. Marriage Is The Leading Cause Of Divorce. - Groucho Marx

28. There's A Method In My Madness.- William Shakespeare

29. Look With Your Eyes Not Your Hands.

30. Yes Sir, No Sir, May I Kiss Your Ass Sir.

31. What Doesn't Kill You Will Make You Stronger. - Friedrick Nietzsche

32. I'm Old Enough To Know Better, Young Enough To Try.

33. How Dry I Am, How Wet I'll Be If I Don't Find The Bathroom Key: I Found The Key, Now Where's The Door, Oh Mommy Dear, I Peed The Floor.

34. The Road To Hell Is Paved With Good Intentions.

35. The Devil's In The Details.

36. All That Glitters Is Not Gold. - William Shakespeare

37. Give Me A Fish And I'll Eat For A Day; Teach Me To Fish And I'll Feast For A Lifetime.

38. Don't Break Your Arm Patting Yourself On The Back.

39. Believe Only Half Of What You See And Nothing Of What You Hear. - Edgar Allen Poe

40. Company Is Like Fish: After Three Days It Begins To Stink. - Benjamin Franklin

41. It's Better To Be Pissed Off Than Pissed On.- Eva Jefferson

42. Go Placidly Amid The Noise And Haste, And Remember What Peace There May Be In Silence. As Far As Possible, Without Surrender, Be On Good Terms With All Persons. - Max Ehrmann

43. Build A Better Mousetrap And The World Will Beat A Path To Your Door. - Ralph Waldo Emerson

44. GIGO- Garbage In Garbage Out.

45. The Quality Of A Person's Life Is In Direct Proportion To Their Commitment To Excellence, Regardless Of Their Chosen Field Of Endeavor. – Vince Lombardi

46. If Your Hose Is Too Short Or Your Pump Is Too Weak, Just Take A Step Forward And You'll Piss On Your Feet. - The Restroom Wall

RE: Fools and Being Foolish

47. Don't Be Penny Wise And Pound Foolish. - Robert Burton

48. Be Brave, Be Daring, And Be Foolish.

49. Fool Me Once Shame On You; Fool Me Twice, Shame On Me.

50. To The Foolish, Every Utterance Of Nonsense Seems Like Wisdom.- Benjamin Disraeli

51. The Fool Wonders, The Wise Man Asks. - Dr. Samuel Johnson

52. Tis Better To Remain Silent And Be Thought A Fool Than Open Ones Mouth And Remove All Doubt. - Abraham Lincoln

Favorite Bumper Stickers By Others
1. Buy Locally Drink Yocally
2. Live To Ride Ride To Live
3. Honk If Parts Fall Off
4. Jesus Loves You Everyone Else Thinks You're An Asshole
5. Humankind Be Both
6. Good Girls Go To Heaven Bad Girls Go Everywhere
7. Florida Sunshine State Arrive Stoned
8. Hate Is Not A Family Value
9. Cash Grass Or Ass Nobody Rides For Free
10. If This Vans A Rockin' Don't Come A Knockin'
11. Cycles Have Equal Rights

12. You Can Play With My Money You Can Play With My Wife But If You Play With My Bike (Motorcycle) You Play With Your Life

13. RE: Motorcycle Helmets- Let Those Who Ride Decide

14. You Can Always Recognize A Happy Biker By The Bugs Between His Teeth

15. Baby I'm Bored

16. I Love TOFU

17. The Bigger The Boys The Bigger The Toys

18. Mess With Me And You Mess With The Whole Trailer Park

19. Make Love Not War

20. Nice Car Sorry About Your Penis

21. Reality Is For People Who Can't Handle Drugs

22. Are You Part Of The Problem Or Part Of The Solution

23. Don't Kick The Can Down The Road

24. My Parents Think I'm Still In College

25. Born On A Mountain Raised In A Cave Partying And Rocking Is All I Crave

26. Watch Out For That Idiot Behind Me

27. I Used To Be All Messed Up On Drugs But Now I'm All Messed Up On The Lord

Made in the USA
Monee, IL
04 January 2020

19847826R00125